POPE BENEDICT XVI

MARY

Spiritual Thoughts Series

Introduction to Volume One by Fr. Ermes Maria Ronchi, OSM
Preface to Volume Two by Cardinal Angelo Comastri
Introduction to Volume Two by Edmond Caruana, OCarm

United States Conference of Catholic Bishops
Washington, D.C.

Cover photo: *L'Osservatore Romano*

First printing, September 2008

ISBN: 978-1-60137-054-9

CONTENTS

⇒≫≫–

VOLUME ONE

INTRODUCTION

iving tent of the Word. With this image epitomizing biblical memory and expressive beauty, Pope Benedict XVI evokes the core of holy Mary's historic journey in his typical language (Homily, May 26, 2005). She is the humble tent of the Word, moved only by the wind of the Spirit, in whom God's coming toward us has its end and resting place.

This collection of Marian thoughts edited by Lucio Coco outlines a pleasant narrative teaching that follows Mary's pilgrimage: urged on throughout her entire life by that first joyous prophecy, *kaire*, *rejoice*; daily faithful to the resounding echo of the "yes" of the Annunciation.

The choice made draws out the newest and most effective characteristics of Benedict's unique language: sobriety, clarity, and beauty. The discussion on Mary is brief, but an essential point is not lacking. He is precise about Mary's strategic position in theology: the meaning of her life is that it "proclaims the greatness of the Lord" (Lk 1:46), not carrying out her own plans but being part of a higher design. He reawakens attention to beauty, a powerful instrument for sensing and communicating, which is the strength in the heart that creates all communion and "re-enchants" life.

And you will find continual references to Mary, the joyful believer, who by the first word of the Angel was already linked to joy, which is an essential name for Christianity and one of the names for the Kingdom (Rm 14:17), as well as one of the names for man; it is far from the false and sad forms of asceticism that divide body and spirit, mind and heart.

For all the faithful, then, calling on Mary as the joyful believer means feeling one's life consoled.

Living tent of the Word: Mary, the place of the encounter between the human and the divine, the bond at the crossroads of time and eternity. These words contain the Pontiff's tireless emphasis on the vital connection between God and man: more divinity means more humanity; *man is great only if God is great*. Holy Mary, *woman of courage and surprise*, shows this human expansion in her existence, an expanded heart that is given to those who live the fullness of Christianity. And this is not all, because in this exchange of gifts a new and incisive expression affirms that now, with the Assumption of Mary, *Heaven has a heart*.

Biblical memory of Mary begins in a house where an Angel speaks, and ends in a house, the upper room in Jerusalem, where fire and wind speak: in she who is *home to the Word* and "*'at home' with God's Word*" (Homily, August 15, 2005), each person rediscovers him- or herself as the tent where homeless Mercy seeks a home. The *Virgin whose heart was open* (Angelus, September 10, 2006) shows that God is not deserved, but welcomed.

Mary, the Church in her nascent state, becomes the teacher of Christianity: with a very effective expression Pope Benedict affirms that Mary, "*through the long, ordinary years of the hidden life, as she brought up Jesus . . . looked on Jesus, she 'learned' him moment by moment.*"

"Let Mary guide you as you 'learn' Jesus" (Address, May 26, 2006).

Going to Mary is therefore going to *Christianity school*, learning the alphabet of faith and hope from her.

"Mary" is one of the words most filled with hope. And with charity. Charity that enters into actions in its entirety, that goes to the heart of things with a regal stride, that does not protect but exposes, unarmed and yet extremely powerful.

The prayers to Mary that conclude this collection also recount a dynamic presence and not a static and abstract image: just as she devoted herself to the event of Christ, so she now devotes herself to the Christian event. She looks after us in God's eternity as a sister who has gone ahead, who precedes us but at the same time awaits us, who slows her pace to the rate of ours to avoid leaving us behind. In the footsteps of Mary, imagining and living our faith as an open and integral system, and not a closed one, becomes a source of strength.

In Mary, the small and the infinite meet: in the events of daily life, in looking on things with awestruck eyes, in love under total silence, in the poetry of familiar gestures, in hope beneath all fears, in the instant that shines for eternity and the eternity that penetrates the instant, she "*wants . . . to teach us a way of life in which God is acknowledged as the center of all there is*" (Angelus, September 10, 2006), she wants to teach us not to live without mystery. Because those who find God will find the fullness of life.

The promise of the Angel is very tangible: "*you will conceive in your womb and bear a son.*" Mary is the authoritative witness that God enters into life and transforms it. In her, in her body—the place where the heart is said to be—the lines of the visible and invisible in the history of Salvation meet one another.

In her body she is the crossroads, one of the places of the encounter between the material reality of life and God. In her body and in her faith, Mary tirelessly points to the center of the faith: Jesus Christ, the shining witness that God comes and transforms body and life, that divinity comes and makes humanity blossom.

Fr. Ermes Maria Ronchi, OSM

MARY

1. *Holy Mary*

We do not praise God sufficiently by keeping silent about his saints, especially Mary, "the Holy One" who became his dwelling place on earth. The simple and multiform light of God appears to us exactly in its variety and richness only in the countenance of the saints, who are the true mirrors of his light. And it is precisely by looking at Mary's face that we can see more clearly than in any other way the beauty, goodness and mercy of God. In her face we can truly perceive the divine light.

> *Homily on the Solemnity of the Assumption*
> *August 15, 2006*

I. THE ANNUNCIATION

2. *The Virgin of Advent*

At a crucial time in history, Mary offered herself, her body and soul, to God as a dwelling place. In her and from her the Son of God took flesh. Through her the Word was made flesh (cf. Jn 1:14). Thus, it is Mary who tells us what Advent is: going forth to meet the Lord who comes to meet us; waiting for him, listening to him, looking at him. Mary tells us why church buildings exist: they exist so that room may be made within us for the Word of God; so that within us and through us the Word may also be made flesh today.

Homily at Our Lady Star of Evangelization Parish, Rome
December 10, 2006

3. *The Immaculate Conception*

In today's consumer society, this period [of Advent] has unfortunately suffered a sort of commercial "pollution" that risks changing its authentic spirit, marked by recollection, moderation and joy, which is not external but intimate. It is thus providential that almost as a portal to Christmas there should be the feast of the one who is the Mother of Jesus and who, better than anyone else, can lead us to know, love and adore the Son of God made man. Let us therefore allow her to accompany us; may her sentiments prompt us to prepare ourselves with heartfelt sincerity and openness of spirit to recognize in the Child of Bethlehem the Son of God who came into the world for our redemption. Let us walk together with her in prayer and accept the repeated invitation that the Advent liturgy addresses to us to remain in expectation—watchful and joyful expectation—for the Lord will not delay: he comes to set his people free from sin.

Angelus
December 11, 2005

4. *In God's hands*

This is something we should indeed learn on the day of the Immaculate Conception: the person who abandons himself totally in God's hands does not become God's puppet, a boring "yes man"; he does not lose his freedom. Only the person who entrusts himself totally to God finds true freedom, the great, creative immensity of the freedom of good. The person who turns to God does not become smaller but greater, for through God and with God he becomes great, he becomes divine, he becomes truly himself. The person who puts himself in God's hands does not distance himself from others, withdrawing into his private salvation; on the contrary, it is only then that his heart truly awakens and he becomes a sensitive, hence, benevolent and open person.

Homily on the fortieth anniversary of the
closing of the Second Vatican Council
December 8, 2005

5. *Listening*

"Reverential hearing": this attitude was typical of Mary Most Holy, as the icon of the Annunciation symbolically portrays: the Virgin receives the heavenly Messenger while she is intent on meditating upon the Sacred Scriptures, usually shown by a book that Mary holds in her hand, on her lap or on a lectern. . . . Mary . . . [is] a humble handmaid of the divine Word.

Angelus
November 6, 2005

6. *The example*

The Virgin is the One who continues to listen, always ready to do the Lord's will; she is an example for the believer who lives in search of God.

Angelus
December 4, 2005

7. *Hail, Mary*

The first word on which I would like to meditate with you is the Angel's greeting to Mary. In the Italian translation the Angel says: "Hail, Mary." But the Greek word below, "*Kaire*," means in itself "be glad" or "rejoice." . . . This is the first word that resounds in the New Testament as such, because the Angel's announcement to Zechariah of the birth of John the Baptist is the word that still rings out on the threshold between the two Testaments. It is only with this dialogue which the Angel Gabriel has with Mary that the New Testament really begins. We can therefore say that the first word of the New Testament is an invitation to joy: "rejoice, be glad!" The New Testament is truly "Gospel," the "Good News" that brings us joy. God is not remote from us, unknown, enigmatic or perhaps dangerous. God is close to us, so close that he makes himself a child and we can informally address this God.

Homily at Santa Maria Consolatrice Parish, Rome
December 18, 2005

8. *Full of grace (1)*

"*Full of grace*" . . . is Mary's most beautiful name, the name God himself gave to her to indicate that she has always been and will always be the *beloved*, the elect, the one chosen to welcome the most precious gift, Jesus: "the incarnate love of God" (Pope Benedict XVI, *Deus Caritas Est*, no. 12).

Angelus
December 8, 2006

9. *Full of grace (2)*

"Full of grace—*gratia plena*," which in the original Greek is *kecharitōménē* . . . "beloved" of God (cf. Lk 1:28) . . . is a title expressed in passive form, but this "passivity" of Mary, who has always been and is for ever "loved" by the Lord, implies her free consent, her personal and original response: in *being loved*, in receiving the gift of God, Mary is fully *active*, because she accepts with personal generosity the wave of God's love poured out upon her. In this too, she is the perfect disciple of her Son, who realizes the fullness of his freedom and thus exercises the freedom through obedience to the Father.

Homily on the Solemnity of the Annunciation
March 25, 2006

10. *The Lord is with you*

God, who became present here on earth, truly dwells in Mary. Mary becomes his tent. What all the cultures desire—that God dwell among us—is brought about here. St. Augustine says: "Before conceiving the Lord in her body she had already conceived him in her soul." She had made room for the Lord in her soul and thus really became the true Temple where God made himself incarnate, where he became present on this earth.

Homily on the Solemnity of the Assumption
August 15, 2006

11. *The tent of the Lord*

Mary, Mother of the Lord, truly teaches us what entering into communion with Christ is: Mary offered her own flesh, her own blood to Jesus and became a living tent of the Word, allowing herself to be penetrated by his presence in body and spirit. Let us pray to her, our holy Mother, so that she may help us to open our entire being, always more, to Christ's presence; so that she may help us to follow him faithfully, day after day, on the streets of our life.

Homily on the Solemnity of Corpus Christi
May 26, 2005

12. *"Do not be afraid, Mary" (Lk 1:30)*

"Do not fear, Mary," [the Angel] says. In fact, there was reason for her to fear, for it was a great burden to bear the weight of the world upon herself, to be the Mother of the universal King, to be the Mother of the Son of God: what a burden that was! It was too heavy a burden for human strength to bear! But the Angel said: "Do not fear! Yes, you are carrying God, but God is carrying you. Do not fear!"

Homily at Santa Maria Consolatrice Parish, Rome
December 18, 2005

13. *And in the hour of our death*

"Do not fear": Mary also addresses these words to us. . . . This world of ours is a world of fear: the fear of misery and poverty, the fear of illness and suffering, the fear of solitude, the fear of death. We have in this world a widely developed insurance system; it is good that it exists. But we know that at the moment of deep suffering, at the moment of the ultimate loneliness of death, no insurance policy will be able to protect us. The only valid insurance in those moments is the one that comes to us from the Lord, who also assures us: "Do not fear, I am always with you." We can fall, but in the end we fall into God's hands, and God's hands are good hands.

Homily at Santa Maria Consolatrice Parish, Rome
December 18, 2005

14. *Behold the servant of the Lord*

Mary belonged to that part of the People of Israel who in Jesus' time were waiting with heartfelt expectation for the Savior's coming. . . . She could not, however, have imagined how this coming would be brought about. Perhaps she expected a coming in glory. The moment when the Archangel Gabriel entered her house and told her that the Lord, the Savior, wanted to take flesh in her, wanted to bring about his coming through her, must have been all the more surprising to her. We can imagine the Virgin's apprehension. Mary, with a tremendous act of faith and obedience, said "yes": "I am the servant of the Lord." And so it was that she became the "dwelling place" of the Lord, a true "temple" in the world and a "door" through which the Lord entered upon the earth.

Homily at First Vespers, First Sunday of Advent
November 26, 2005

15. *Woman of hope*

Mary is a woman of hope: only because she believes in God's promises and awaits the salvation of Israel, can the angel visit her and call her to the decisive service of these promises.

Encyclical letter God Is Love (Deus Caritas Est), *no. 41*
December 25, 2005

16. *Let it be done to me according to your Word*

At the end of the colloquium, Mary answered the Angel, "I am the servant of the Lord. Let it be done to me as you say." Thus, Mary anticipated the Our Father's third invocation: "Your will be done." She said "yes" to God's great will, a will apparently too great for a human being; Mary said "yes" to this divine will, she placed herself within this will, placed her whole life with a great "yes" within God's will, and thus opened the world's door to God. Adam and Eve, with their "no" to God's will, had closed this door. "Let God's will be done": Mary invites us too to say this "yes" which sometimes seems so difficult. We are tempted to prefer our own will, but she tells us: "Be brave, you too say: 'Your will be done,' because this will is good." It might at first seem an unbearable burden, a yoke impossible to bear; but in reality, God's will is not a burden, God's will gives us wings to fly high and thus we too can dare, with Mary, to open the door of our lives to God, the doors of this world, by saying "yes" to his will, aware that this will is the true good and leads us to true happiness.

Homily at Santa Maria Consolatrice Parish, Rome
December 18, 2005

17. *Handmaid of the Lord*

[Mary] is and remains the handmaid of the Lord who does not put herself at the center, but wants to lead us towards God, to teach us a way of life in which God is acknowledged as the center of all there is and the center of our personal lives.

Angelus
September 10, 2006

18. *Giving oneself entirely*

[Mary] is, so to speak, totally emptied of herself; she has given herself entirely to Christ and with him is given as a gift to us all. Indeed, the more the human person gives himself, the more he finds himself.

Homily on the fortieth anniversary of the
closing of the Second Vatican Council
December 8, 2005

19. *Dwelling place in Heaven*

We can praise Mary, we can venerate Mary for she is "blessed," she is blessed for ever. . . . She is blessed because she is united to God, she lives with God and in God. On the eve of his Passion, taking leave of his disciples, the Lord said: "In my Father's house are many rooms . . . I go to prepare a place for you." By saying, "I am the handmaid of the Lord; let it be done to me according to your word," Mary prepared God's dwelling here on earth; with her body and soul, she became his dwelling place and thereby opened the earth to heaven.

Homily at Mass for the Solemnity of the Assumption
August 15, 2006

20. *Flame of love*

[Mary teaches that] to love according to God it is necessary to live in him and of him: God is the first "home" of human beings, and only by dwelling in God do men and women burn with a flame of divine love that can set the world "on fire."

Message for the Eightieth World Mission Sunday
April 29, 2006

21. *The call*

Mary received her vocation from the lips of an angel. The Angel does not enter our room visibly, but the Lord has a plan for each of us, he calls each one of us by name. Our task is to learn how to listen, to perceive his call, to be courageous and faithful in following him and, when all is said and done, to be found trustworthy servants who have used well the gifts given us.

Homily at Vespers with the religious and
seminarians of Bavaria
September 11, 2006

II. The Visitation

22. *Visiting*

Mary went to see her elderly cousin Elizabeth, whom everyone said was sterile but who instead had reached the sixth month of a pregnancy given to her by God (cf. Lk 1:36), carrying in her womb the recently conceived Jesus. She was a young girl but she was not afraid, for God was with her, within her. . . . Jesus' presence filled her with the Holy Spirit. When she entered Elizabeth's house, her greeting was overflowing with grace: John leapt in his mother's womb, as if he were aware of the coming of the One whom he would one day proclaim to Israel. The children exulted, the mothers exulted. This meeting, imbued with the joy of the Holy Spirit, is expressed in the Canticle of the *Magnificat*.

Address at the conclusion of the Marian month
May 31, 2005

23. *Mary and Elizabeth*

How can we fail to see that the hidden protagonist in the meeting between the young Mary and the by-then elderly Elizabeth is Jesus? Mary bears him in her womb as in a sacred tabernacle and offers him as the greatest gift to Zechariah, to Elizabeth, his wife, and also to the infant developing in her womb. "Behold," the Mother of John the Baptist says, "when the voice of your greeting came to my ears, the babe in my womb leaped for joy" (Lk 1:44). Whoever opens his or her heart to the Mother encounters and welcomes the Son and is pervaded by his joy.

Address at the conclusion of the Marian month
May 31, 2006

24. *Woman of faith*

Elizabeth, the mother of John the Baptist, had reserved the first beatitude of the Gospel [for Mary]: "Blessed are you who believed that what was spoken to you by the Lord would be fulfilled" (Lk 1:45). Mary is the "believer" par excellence, the pure and perfect disciple.

General Audience
February 15, 2006

25. *The journey of joy*

Joy must always be shared. Joy must be communicated. Mary went without delay to communicate her joy to her cousin Elizabeth. . . . This is the real commitment of Advent: to bring joy to others. Joy is the true gift of Christmas, not expensive presents that demand time and money. We can transmit this joy simply: with a smile, with a kind gesture, with some small help, with forgiveness. Let us give this joy and the joy given will be returned to us. Let us seek in particular to communicate the deepest joy, that of knowing God in Christ. Let us pray that this presence of God's liberating joy will shine out in our lives.

Homily at Santa Maria Consolatrice Parish, Rome
December 18, 2005

26. *Bringing Jesus*

Yes, welcoming Jesus and bringing him to others is the true joy of Christians! Dear Brothers and Sisters, let us follow and imitate Mary, a deeply Eucharistic soul, and our whole life can become a *Magnificat* (cf. Pope John Paul II, *Ecclesia de Eucharistia*, no. 58), praise of God. May this be the grace that we ask from the Virgin Most Holy.

Address at the conclusion of the Marian month
May 31, 2005

27. *Eucharistic existence*

At the school of Mary, "Woman of the Eucharist," as the late Pope John Paul II loved to call her, we welcome Jesus' living presence in ourselves to bring him to everyone by loving service. Let us learn to always live in communion with the Crucified and Risen Christ, allowing ourselves to be led by his and our heavenly Mother. In this way, nourished by the Word and Bread of Life, our existence will become entirely Eucharistic and thanks will be given to the Father through Christ in the Holy Spirit.

Angelus
May 29, 2005

28. *Model of the Church*

The first thing that Mary did after receiving the Angel's message was to go "in haste" to the house of her cousin Elizabeth in order to be of service to her (cf. Lk 1:39). The Virgin's initiative was one of genuine charity; it was humble and courageous, motivated by faith in God's Word and the inner promptings of the Holy Spirit. Those who love forget about themselves and place themselves at the service of their neighbor. Here we have the image and model of the Church! Every Ecclesial Community, like the Mother of Christ, is called to accept with total generosity the mystery of God who comes to dwell within her and guides her steps in the ways of love.

Homily at the consistory for the creation of new cardinals
March 25, 2006

III. The Magnificat

29. *My soul magnifies the Lord*

Outstanding among the saints is Mary, Mother of the Lord and mirror of all holiness. In the Gospel of Luke we find her engaged in a service of charity to her cousin Elizabeth, with whom she remained for "about three months" (Lk 1:56) so as to assist her in the final phase of her pregnancy. "*Magnificat anima mea Dominum*," she says on the occasion of that visit, "My soul magnifies the Lord" (Lk 1:46). In these words she expresses her whole program of life: not setting herself at the center, but leaving space for God, who is encountered both in prayer and in service of neighbor—only then does goodness enter the world. Mary's greatness consists in the fact that she wants to magnify God, not herself. She is lowly: her only desire is to be the handmaid of the Lord (cf. Lk 1:38, 48). She knows that she will only contribute to the salvation of the world if, rather than carrying out her own projects, she places herself completely at the disposal of God's initiatives.

Encyclical letter God Is Love (Deus Caritas Est), *no. 41*
December 25, 2005

30. *My soul proclaims the greatness of the Lord*

In the Gospel we heard the *Magnificat*, that great poem inspired by the Holy Spirit that came from Mary's lips, indeed, from Mary's heart. This marvelous canticle mirrors the entire soul, the entire personality of Mary. We can say that this hymn of hers is a portrait of Mary, a true icon in which we can see her exactly as she is. . . . It begins with the word "*Magnificat*": my soul "magnifies" the Lord, that is, "proclaims the greatness" of the Lord. Mary wanted God to be great in the world, great in her life and present among us all. She was not afraid that God might be a "rival" in our life, that with his greatness he might encroach on our freedom, our vital space. She knew that if God is great, we too are great. Our life is not oppressed but raised and expanded: it is precisely then that it becomes great in the splendor of God. . . . Only if God is great is humankind also great. With Mary, we must begin to understand that this is so.

> *Homily on the Solemnity of the Assumption*
> *August 15, 2005*

31. *Thinking with God*

Mary's poem—the *Magnificat*—is quite original; yet at the same time, it is a "fabric" woven throughout of "threads" from the Old Testament, of words of God. Thus, we see that Mary was, so to speak, "at home" with God's word, she lived on God's word, she was penetrated by God's word.

To the extent that she spoke with God's words, she thought with God's words, her thoughts were God's thoughts, her words, God's words. She was penetrated by divine light and this is why she was so resplendent, so good, so radiant with love and goodness. Mary lived on the Word of God, she was imbued with the Word of God. And the fact that she was immersed in the Word of God and was totally familiar with the Word also endowed her later with the inner enlightenment of wisdom. Whoever thinks with God thinks well, and whoever speaks to God speaks well. They have valid criteria to judge all the things of the world. They become prudent, wise, and at the same time good; they also become strong and courageous with the strength of God, who resists evil and fosters good in the world.

Homily on the Solemnity of the Assumption
August 15, 2005

32. *Dwelling of the Word*

[Mary] lives her whole life in the Word of God. It is as though she were steeped in the Word. Thus, all her thoughts, her will and her actions are imbued with and formed by the Word. Since she herself dwells in the Word, she can also become the new "Dwelling Place" of the Word in the world.

Address at the conclusion of the papal spiritual exercises
March 11, 2006

33. *Willing with God*

The *Magnificat*—a portrait, so to speak, of [Mary's] soul—is entirely woven from threads of Holy Scripture, threads drawn from the Word of God. Here we see how completely at home Mary is with the Word of God, with ease she moves in and out of it. She speaks and thinks with the Word of God; the Word of God becomes her word, and her word issues from the Word of God. Here we see how her thoughts are attuned to the thoughts of God, how her will is one with the will of God.

Encyclical letter God Is Love (Deus Caritas Est)*, no. 41*
December 25, 2005

34. *Woman of love*

"Mary . . . is a woman who loves. . . . As a believer who in faith thinks with God's thoughts and wills with God's will, she cannot fail to be a woman who loves" (Pope Benedict XVI, *Deus Caritas Est*, no. 41). Yes, dear brothers and sisters, Mary is the fruit and sign of the love God has for us, of his tenderness and mercy. Therefore, together with our brothers in the faith of all times and all places, we turn to her in our needs and hopes, in the joyful and sorrowful events of life.

Address at the Shrine of Our Lady of Divine Love
May 1, 2006

35. *Daring with God*

[Mary's] heart was enlarged by being and feeling together with God. In her, God's goodness came very close to us. Mary thus stands before us as a sign of comfort, encouragement and hope. She turns to us, saying: "Have the courage to dare with God! Try it! Do not be afraid of him! Have the courage to risk with faith! Have the courage to risk with goodness! Have the courage to risk with a pure heart! Commit yourselves to God, then you will see that it is precisely by doing so that your life will become broad and light, not boring but filled with infinite surprises, for God's infinite goodness is never depleted!"

> *Homily on the fortieth anniversary of the*
> *closing of the Second Vatican Council*
> *December 8, 2005*

36. *The humility of Mary*

Why exactly did God choose from among all women Mary of Nazareth? The answer is hidden in the unfathomable mystery of the divine will. There is one reason, however, which is highlighted in the Gospel: her humility. . . . In the *Magnificat*, her canticle of praise, the Virgin herself says: "My soul magnifies the Lord . . . because he looked upon his servant in her lowliness" (Lk 1:46, 48). Yes, God was attracted by the humility of Mary, who found favor in his eyes (cf. Lk 1:30). She thus became the Mother of God, the image and model of the Church, chosen among the peoples to receive the Lord's blessing and communicate it to the entire human family.

Angelus
December 8, 2006

37. *The Marian praises*

In the *Magnificat*, the great hymn of Our Lady . . . we find some surprising words. Mary says: "Henceforth all generations will call me blessed." The Mother of the Lord prophesies the Marian praises of the Church for all of the future, the Marian devotion of the People of God until the end of time. In praising Mary, the Church did not invent something "adjacent" to Scripture: she responded to this prophecy which Mary made at that moment of grace.

Homily on the Solemnity of the Assumption
August 15, 2006

IV. THE NATIVITY

38. *Christmas*

To transform the world, God chose a humble young girl from a village in Galilee, Mary of Nazareth, and challenged her with this greeting: "Hail, full of grace, the Lord is with you." In these words lies the secret of an authentic Christmas. God repeats them to the Church, to each one of us: Rejoice, the Lord is close! With Mary's help, let us offer ourselves with humility and courage so that the world may accept Christ, who is the source of true joy.

Angelus
December 17, 2006

39. *The motherhood of Mary*

The mother is the one who gives life but also who helps and teaches how to live. Mary is a Mother, the Mother of Jesus, to whom she gave her blood and her body. And it is she who presents to us the eternal Word of the Father, who came to dwell among us.

Homily at First Vespers, Solemnity of Mary,
Mother of God
December 31, 2005

40. Theotokos *(The Mother of God)*

[In the Letter to the Galatians] St. Paul said: "God sent forth his Son, born of woman" (Gal 4:4). Origen commented: "Note well that he did not say, 'born *by means of* a woman' but 'born *of* a woman'" (*Comment on the Letter to the Galatians, PG* 14, 1298). This acute observation of the great exegete and ecclesiastical writer is important: in fact, if the Son of God had been born only "by means of" a woman, he would not truly have taken on our humanity, something which instead he did by taking flesh "of" Mary. Mary's motherhood, therefore, is true and fully human. The fundamental truth about Jesus as a divine Person who fully assumed our human nature is condensed in the phrase: "God sent forth his Son born of woman." He is the Son of God, he is generated by God and *at the same time* he is the son of a woman, Mary. He comes from her. He is *of* God and *of* Mary. For this reason one can and must call the Mother of Jesus the Mother of God [in Greek, *Theotokos*].

> *Homily at First Vespers, Solemnity of Mary,*
> *Mother of God*
> *December 31, 2006*

41. *"Glory to God in the highest . . ." (Lk 2:14)*

"Hail, Holy Mother," the liturgy sings, "the Child to whom you gave birth is the King of Heaven and Earth for ever." The Angels' proclamation at Bethlehem resounds in Mary's motherly heart, filling it with wonder: "Glory to God in high heaven, peace on earth to those on whom his favor rests" (Lk 2:14). And the Gospel adds that Mary "treasured all these things and reflected on them in her heart" (Lk 2:19). Like Mary, the Church also treasures and reflects upon the Word of God, comparing it to the various changing situations she encounters on her way.

Angelus
January 1, 2006

42. *". . . and on earth peace to those on whom his favor rests" (Lk 2:14)*

Who are those whom God loves, and why does he love them? Does God have favorites? Does he love only certain people, while abandoning the others to themselves? The Gospel answers these questions by pointing to some particular people whom God loves. . . . Mary, Joseph, Elizabeth, Zechariah, Simeon and Anna. . . . the shepherds and the Wise Men from the East, the "Magi." . . . [are] people who were watchful. . . . ready to receive God's Word through the Angel's proclamation. Their life was not closed in on itself; their hearts were open. In some way, deep down, they were waiting for something; they were waiting for God. Their watchfulness was a kind of readiness—a readiness to listen and to set out. They were waiting for a light which would show them the way. That is what is important for God. He loves everyone, because everyone is his creature. But some persons have closed their hearts; there is no door by which his love can enter. They think that they do not need God, nor do they want him. Other persons, who, from a moral standpoint, are perhaps no less wretched and sinful, at least experience a certain remorse. They are waiting for God. They realize that they need his goodness, even if they have no clear idea of what this means. Into their expectant hearts God's light can enter, and with it, his peace. God seeks persons who can be vessels and heralds of his peace. Let us pray that he will not find our hearts closed. Let us strive to be active heralds of his peace—in the world of today.

Homily at Midnight Mass, Solemnity of the
Nativity of the Lord
December 24, 2005

43. *Virgin Mother*

The Christian community, which in these days has remained in prayerful adoration before the crib, looks with particular love to the Virgin Mary, identifying itself with her while contemplating the newborn Baby, wrapped in swaddling clothes and laid in a manger. Like Mary, the Church also remains in silence in order to welcome and keep the interior resonances of the Word made flesh and in order not to lose the divine-human warmth that radiates from his presence. [It is a blessing of God!] The Church, like the Virgin, does none other than show Jesus, the Savior, to everyone, and reflects to each one the light of his face, the splendor of goodness and truth.

Angelus
January 1, 2007

44. *Bringing forth Christ*

"If, according to the flesh, the Mother of Christ is one alone, according to the faith all souls bring forth Christ; each, in fact, welcomes the Word of God within . . ." (St. Ambrose, *Exposition of the Holy Gospel According to St. Luke*, 2:26-27). . . . Thus, interpreting Our Lady's very words, the Holy Doctor invites us to ensure that the Lord can find a dwelling place in our own souls and lives. Not only must we carry him in our hearts, but we must bring him to the world, so that we too can bring forth Christ for our epoch. Let us pray the Lord to help us praise him with Mary's spirit and soul, and to bring Christ back to our world.

General Audience
February 15, 2006

45. *Spiritual Incarnation*

"In the first [coming]," St. Bernard wrote, "Christ was our redemption; in the last coming he will reveal himself to us as our life: in this lies our repose and consolation" (*Discourse 5 on Advent*, 1). The archetype for that coming of Christ, which we might call a "spiritual incarnation," is always Mary. Just as the Virgin Mother pondered in her heart on the Word made flesh, so every individual soul and the entire Church are called during their earthly pilgrimage to wait for Christ who comes and to welcome him with faith and love ever new.

Homily at First Vespers, First Sunday of Advent
December 2, 2006

46. *Vocation and mission*

[Mary] welcomed Jesus with faith and gave him to the world with love. This is also our vocation and our mission, the vocation and mission of the Church: to welcome Christ into our lives and give him to the world, so "that the world might be saved through him" (Jn 3:17).

Angelus
December 8, 2006

47. *The face of the Child*

May Mary help us to recognize in the face of the Child of Bethlehem, conceived in her virginal womb, the divine Redeemer who came into the world to reveal to us the authentic face of God.

Angelus
December 4, 2005

48. *The face of God*

Who can accompany us better on this demanding journey of holiness than Mary? Who can teach us to adore Christ better than she? May she help especially the new generations to recognize the true face of God in Christ and to worship, love and serve him with total dedication.

Angelus
August 7, 2005

49. *Epiphany of the Lord*

"How can this come about?", we also ask ourselves with the words that the Virgin addresses to the Archangel Gabriel. And she herself, the Mother of Christ and of the Church, gives us the answer: with her example of total availability to God's will—"*fiat mihi secundum verbum tuum*" ["May it be done to me according to your word"] (Lk 1:38)—she teaches us to be a "manifestation" of the Lord, opening our hearts to the power of grace and faithfully abiding by the words of her Son, light of the world and the ultimate end of history.

Homily on the Solemnity of the Epiphany
January 6, 2006

50. *Presentation of Jesus in the Temple*

The first person to be associated with Christ on the path of obedience, proven faith and shared suffering was his Mother, Mary. The Gospel text portrays her in the act of offering her Son: an unconditional offering that involves her in the first person. Mary is the Mother of the One who is "the glory of [his] people Israel" and a "light for revelation to the Gentiles," but also "a sign that is spoken against" (cf. Lk 2:32, 34). And in her immaculate soul, she herself was to be pierced by the sword of sorrow, thus showing that her role in the history of salvation did not end in the mystery of the Incarnation but was completed in loving and sorrowful participation in the death and Resurrection of her Son. Bringing her Son to Jerusalem, the Virgin Mother offered him to God as a true Lamb who takes away the sins of the world. She held him out to Simeon and Anna as the proclamation of redemption; she presented him to all as a light for a safe journey on the path of truth and love.

Homily on the World Day of Consecrated Life
February 2, 2006

51. *Simeon's prophecy*

The words of the elderly Simeon (Lk 2:34-35) [anticipate, together with salvation,] the contradictory sign of the Cross, and of the sword that beneath the Cross of the Son was to pierce the Mother's soul, thereby making her not only the Mother of God but also Mother of us all.

Address at the Shrine of Our Lady of Divine Love
May 1, 2006

52. *Marian vocations*

We contemplate [Mary] on the Memorial of her Presentation in the Temple as Mother and model of the Church, who welcomes in herself both vocations: to virginity and to marriage, to contemplative life and to active life.

Angelus
November 19, 2006

53. *"His mother kept all these things in her heart" (Lk 2:51)*

The Evangelist Luke describes [Mary] as the silent Virgin who listens constantly to the eternal Word, who lives in the Word of God. Mary treasures in her heart the words that come from God and, piecing them together as in a mosaic, learns to understand them. Let us too, at her school, learn to become attentive and docile disciples of the Lord.

Homily on the Solemnity of Mary, Mother of God
January 1, 2006

54. *Virgin of silence*

Let us ask the Virgin Mary to teach us the secret of silence that becomes praise, of recollection that is conducive to meditation, of love for nature that blossoms in gratitude to God. Thus, we will more easily be able to welcome the light of the Truth into our hearts and practice it in freedom and love.

Angelus
July 17, 2005

V. Disciple of Jesus

55. *In Cana in Galilee*

"They have no wine" (Jn 2:3). Weddings in the Holy Land were celebrated for a whole week; the entire town took part, and consequently much wine was consumed. Now the bride and groom find themselves in trouble, and Mary simply says this to Jesus. She doesn't ask for anything specific, much less that Jesus exercise his power, perform a miracle, produce wine. She simply hands the matter over to Jesus and leaves it to him to decide about what to do. In the simple words of the Mother of Jesus, we can see . . . her affectionate concern for people, that maternal affection which makes her aware of the problems of others. We see her heartfelt goodness and her willingness to help. This is the Mother that generations of people have come [on pilgrimage] to visit. To her we entrust our cares, our needs and our troubles. Her maternal readiness to help, in which we trust, appears here for the first time in the Holy Scriptures.

Homily at Mass in Kapellplatz, Altötting
September 11, 2006

56. *"Do whatever he tells you" (Jn 2:5)*

As we listen to this Gospel passage, it is worth going a little deeper [into the wedding feast at Cana], not only to understand Jesus and Mary better, but also to learn from Mary the right way to pray. Mary does not really ask something of Jesus: she simply says to him: "They have no wine" (Jn 2:3). . . . Mary leaves everything to the Lord's judgment. At Nazareth she gave over her will, immersing it in the will of God: "Here am I, the servant of the Lord; let it be with me according to your word" (Lk 1:38). And this continues to be her fundamental attitude. This is how she teaches us to pray: not by seeking to assert before God our own will and our own desires, however important they may be, however reasonable they might appear to us, but rather to bring them before him and to let him decide what he intends to do. From Mary we learn graciousness and readiness to help, but we also learn humility and generosity in accepting God's will, in the confident conviction that, whatever it may be, it will be our, and my own, true good.

Homily at Mass in Kapellplatz, Altötting
September 11, 2006

57. *Our advocate*

Mary, the Mother of the Lord, has received from the faithful the title of *Advocate*: she is our advocate before God. And this is how we see her, from the wedding-feast of Cana onwards: as a woman who is kindly, filled with maternal concern and love, a woman who is attentive to the needs of others and, out of desire to help them, brings those needs before the Lord.

Homily at Mass in Islinger Feld, Regensburg
September 12, 2006

58. *The intercession of Mary*

After his mother Mary's prayer [in Cana in Galilee], Jesus comes to the aid of the spouses in difficulty, transforming the water into wine. Mary also intercedes with Jesus on our behalf. Her strong faith is our model. We must entrust our requests to her maternal intercession.

Angelus
January 14, 2007

59. *Learning Jesus*

Mary learned from Jesus! From her very first "*fiat*," through the long, ordinary years of the hidden life, as she brought up Jesus, or when in Cana in Galilee she asked for the first sign, or when finally on Calvary, by the Cross, she looked on Jesus, she "learned" him moment by moment. Firstly in faith and then in her womb, she received the Body of Jesus and then gave birth to him. Day after day, enraptured, she adored him. She served him with solicitous love, singing the *Magnificat* in her heart. . . . Let Mary guide you as you "learn" Jesus. Keep your eyes fixed on him. Let him form you.

Address in Częstochowa to religious, seminarians, and
representatives of ecclesial movements
May 26, 2006

60. *Christ at the center*

How necessary it is—both for the lives of individuals and for the serene and peaceful coexistence of all people—to see God as the center of all there is and the center of our personal lives. The supreme example of this attitude is Mary, Mother of the Lord. Throughout her earthly life, she was the Woman who listened, the Virgin whose heart was open towards God and towards others. . . . She is and remains the handmaid of the Lord who does not put herself at the center, but wants to lead us towards God, to teach us a way of life in which God is acknowledged as the center of all there is and the center of our personal lives.

Angelus
September 10, 2006

61. *Public life*

We can imagine how in various situations the Virgin must have pondered on those words [of the Angel: "Do not fear, Mary" (Lk 1:30)], she must have heard them again. At the moment when Simeon said to her: "This child is destined to be the downfall and the rise of many in Israel, a sign that will be opposed—and you yourself will be pierced with a sword," at that very moment in which she might have succumbed to fear, Mary returned to the Angel's words and felt their echo within her: "Do not fear, God is carrying you." Then, when contradictions were unleashed against Jesus during his public life and many said, "He is crazy," she thought once again of the Angel's words in her heart, "Do not fear," and went ahead. Lastly, in the encounter on the way to Calvary and then under the Cross, when all seemed to be destroyed, she again heard the Angel's words in her heart: "Do not fear." Hence, she stood courageously beside her dying Son and, sustained by faith, moved towards the Resurrection, towards Pentecost, towards the foundation of the new family of the Church.

Homily at Santa Maria Consolatrice Parish, Rome
December 18, 2005

62. *Listening to Christ*

The Virgin Mary herself, among all human creatures the closest to God, still had to walk day after day in a pilgrimage of faith (cf. Second Vatican Council, *Lumen Gentium*, no. 58), constantly guarding and meditating on in her heart the Word that God addressed to her through Holy Scripture and through the events of the life of her Son, in whom she recognized and welcomed the Lord's mysterious voice. And so, this is the gift and duty for each one of us . . . to listen to Christ, like Mary. To listen to him in his Word, contained in Sacred Scripture. To listen to him in the events of our lives, seeking to decipher in them the messages of Providence. Finally, to listen to him in our brothers and sisters, especially in the lowly and the poor, to whom Jesus himself demands our concrete love. To listen to Christ and obey his voice: this is the principal way, the only way, that leads to the fullness of joy and of love.

Angelus
March 12, 2006

VI. At the Foot of the Cross

63. *On Calvary*

The traditional image of the Crucifixion . . . portrays the Virgin Mary at the foot of the Cross, according to the description of the Evangelist John, the only one of the Apostles who stayed by the dying Jesus. . . . The Evangelist recounts: Mary was standing by the Cross (cf. Jn 19:25-27). Her sorrow is united with that of her Son. It is a sorrow full of faith and love. The Virgin on Calvary participates in the saving power of the suffering of Christ, joining her "*fiat*," her "yes," to that of her Son.

Angelus
September 17, 2006

64. *Our Lady of Sorrows*

In [Mary], God has impressed his own image, the image of
the One who follows the lost sheep even up into the mountains and among the briars and thornbushes of the sins of
this world, letting himself be spiked by the crown of thorns
of these sins in order to take the sheep on his shoulders and
bring it home. As a merciful Mother, Mary is the anticipated figure and everlasting portrait of the Son. Thus, we
see that the image of the Sorrowful Virgin, of the Mother
who shares her suffering and her love, is also a true image
of the Immaculate Conception.

Homily on the fortieth anniversary of the
closing of the Second Vatican Council
December 8, 2005

65. *The legacy of Jesus*

In [the] Gospel we have heard how the Lord gave Mary as
a Mother to the beloved disciple and, in him, to all of us.
In every age, Christians have received with gratitude this
legacy of Jesus, and, in their recourse to his Mother, they
have always found the security and confident hope which
gives them joy in God and makes us joyful in our faith in
him. May we too receive Mary as the lodestar guiding our
lives, introducing us into the great family of God! Truly,
those who believe are never alone.

Homily at Mass in Islinger Feld, Regensburg
September 12, 2006

66. *Our Mother*

The lives of the saints are not limited to their earthly biographies but also include their being and working in God after death. In the saints one thing becomes clear: those who draw near to God do not withdraw from men, but rather become truly close to them. In no one do we see this more clearly than in Mary. The words addressed by the crucified Lord to his disciple—to John and through him to all disciples of Jesus: "Behold, your mother!" (Jn 19:27)—are fulfilled anew in every generation. Mary has truly become the Mother of all believers. Men and women of every time and place have recourse to her motherly kindness and her virginal purity and grace, in all their needs and aspirations, their joys and sorrows, their moments of loneliness and their common endeavors.

Encyclical letter God Is Love (Deus Caritas Est), *no. 42*
December 25, 2005

67. *The mission of Mary*

Mary's motherhood, which began with her *fiat* in Nazareth, is fulfilled at the foot of the Cross. Although it is true—as St. Anselm says—that "from the moment of her *fiat* Mary began to carry all of us in her womb," the maternal vocation and mission of the Virgin towards those who believe in Christ actually began when Jesus said to her: "Woman, behold your son!" (Jn 19:26).

Homily at Mass in Ephesus
November 29, 2006

68. *Imitation of Mary*

I recommend that you love the Mother of the Lord. Do as St. John did, welcoming her deeply into your own heart. Allow yourselves to be continually renewed by her maternal love. Learn from her how to love Christ.

> *Homily at Mass of Priestly Ordination,*
> *Pentecost Sunday*
> *May 15, 2005*

69. *Mother of sorrows*

One must remain in prayer with Mary, the Mother given to us by Christ from the Cross.

> *Homily at Mass in Verona, Italy*
> *October 19, 2006*

70. *Spiritual mother*

Mary is the *Spiritual Mother of all humanity*, because Jesus on the Cross shed his blood for all of us and from the Cross he entrusted us all to her maternal care.

> *Homily on the Solemnity of Mary, Mother of God*
> *January 1, 2007*

71. *Thrust of the lance*

Mary . . . followed Jesus with total faith when he set out with determination for Jerusalem, to suffer the Passion. She received like a "fresh skin" the "new wine" brought by the Son for the messianic betrothal (cf. Mk 2:22). And so it was that the grace she requested with a motherly instinct for the spouses at Cana, she herself had first received beneath the Cross, poured out from the pierced Heart of the Son, an incarnation of God's love for humanity (cf. Pope Benedict XVI, *Deus Caritas Est*, nos. 13-15).

Angelus
February 26, 2006

72. *The Heart of Mary*

In the Heart of the Redeemer we adore God's love for humanity, his will for universal salvation, his infinite mercy. . . . The heart that resembles that of Christ more than any other is without a doubt the Heart of Mary, his Immaculate Mother.

Angelus
June 5, 2005

73. *Mother of the Church*

Mary, present on Calvary beneath the Cross, is also present with the Church and as Mother of the Church in each one of our Eucharistic Celebrations (cf. Pope John Paul II, *Ecclesia de Eucharistia*, no. 57). No one better than she, therefore, can teach us to understand and live Holy Mass with faith and love, uniting ourselves with Christ's redeeming sacrifice. When we receive Holy Communion, like Mary and united to her, we too clasp the wood that Jesus with his love transformed into an instrument of salvation, and pronounce our "Amen," our "Yes" to Love, crucified and risen.

Angelus
September 11, 2005

74. *Our Lady of Holy Saturday*

On *Holy Saturday* the Church, spiritually united with Mary, remains in prayer at the tomb, where the Body of the Son of God is lying inert as it were in a condition of repose after the creative work of redemption brought about with his death (cf. Heb 4:1-13).

General Audience
April 12, 2006

75. *Following Jesus*

Mary is a woman who loves. How could it be otherwise? As a believer who in faith thinks with God's thoughts and wills with God's will, she cannot fail to be a woman who loves. We sense this in her quiet gestures, as recounted by the infancy narratives in the Gospel. We see it in the delicacy with which she recognizes the need of the spouses at Cana and makes it known to Jesus. We see it in the humility with which she recedes into the background during Jesus' public life, knowing that the Son must establish a new family and that the Mother's hour will come only with the Cross, which will be Jesus' true hour (cf. Jn 2:4; 13:1). When the disciples flee, Mary will remain beneath the Cross (cf. Jn 19:25-27); later, at the hour of Pentecost, it will be they who gather around her as they wait for the Holy Spirit (cf. Acts 1:14).

Encyclical letter God Is Love (Deus Caritas Est), *no. 41*
December 25, 2005

VII. PENTECOST

76. *Eucharistic woman*

Our Lady accompanies us every day in our prayers. . . .
In his last Encyclical, *Ecclesia de Eucharistia*, our beloved
Pope John Paul II presented her to us as "Woman of the
Eucharist" throughout her life (cf. no. 53). "Woman of the
Eucharist" through and through, beginning with her inner
disposition: from the Annunciation, when she offered herself for the Incarnation of the Word of God, to the Cross
and to the Resurrection; "Woman of the Eucharist" in the
period subsequent to Pentecost, when she received in the
Sacrament that Body which she had conceived and carried
in her womb.

> *Address at the conclusion of the Marian month*
> *May 31, 2005*

77. *The Upper Room*

In the Upper Room the Apostles did not know what awaited
them. They were afraid and worried about their own future.
They continued to marvel at the death and resurrection of
Jesus and were in anguish at being left on their own after
his ascension into Heaven. Mary, "she who believed in the

fulfillment of the Lord's words" (cf. Lk 1:45), assiduous in prayer alongside the Apostles, taught perseverance in the faith. By her own attitude she convinced them that the Holy Spirit, in his wisdom, knew well the path on which he was leading them, and that consequently they could place their confidence in God, giving themselves to him unreservedly, with their talents, their limitations and their future.

Address in Częstochowa to religious, seminarians, and representatives of ecclesial movements
May 26, 2006

78. *The mystery of Pentecost*

We contemplate [the Virgin Mary] in the glorious mystery of Pentecost. The Holy Spirit, who at Nazareth descended upon her to make her the Mother of the Word Incarnate (cf. Lk 1:35), descended . . . on the nascent Church joined together around her in the Upper Room (cf. Acts 1:14). We invoke with trust Mary Most Holy, in order to obtain a renewed outpouring of the Spirit on the Church in our days.

Regina Caeli
May 15, 2005

79. *The Virgin of the Upper Room*

As in the Upper Room, the Blessed Virgin always constitutes the living memorial of Jesus. It is she who enlivens their prayers and sustains their hope. Let us ask her to guide us on our daily journey and to protect with special love those Christian communities that live in conditions of greater difficulty and suffering.

Angelus
March 26, 2006

80. *Mother and teacher*

In the days that followed the Lord's Resurrection, the Apostles stayed together, comforted by Mary's presence, and after the Ascension they persevered with her in prayerful expectation of Pentecost. Our Lady was a mother and teacher to them, a role that she continues to play for Christians of all times. Every year, at Eastertide, we relive this experience more intensely and, perhaps precisely for this reason, popular tradition has dedicated to Mary the month of May that normally falls between Easter and Pentecost. Consequently, this month . . . helps us to rediscover the maternal role that she plays in our lives so that we may always be docile disciples and courageous witnesses of the Risen Lord.

Regina Caeli
April 30, 2006

81. *Mary and the Trinity*

The Virgin Mary, among all creatures, is a masterpiece of the Most Holy Trinity. In her humble heart full of faith, God prepared a worthy dwelling place for himself in order to bring to completion the mystery of salvation. Divine Love found perfect correspondence in her, and in her womb the Only-Begotten Son was made man. Let us turn to Mary with filial trust, so that with her help we may progress in love and make our life a hymn of praise to the Father through the Son in the Holy Spirit.

Angelus
June 11, 2006

VIII. The Assumption

82. *Heart of Heaven*

Mary was taken up body and soul into Heaven: there is even room in God for the body. Heaven is no longer a very remote sphere unknown to us. We have a mother in Heaven. And the Mother of God, the Mother of the Son of God, is our Mother. He himself has said so. He made her our Mother when he said to the disciple and to all of us: "Behold, your Mother!" We have a Mother in Heaven. Heaven is open, Heaven has a heart.

> *Homily on the Solemnity of the Assumption*
> *August 15, 2005*

83. *Nearness*

Mary is taken up body and soul into the glory of Heaven, and with God and in God she is Queen of Heaven and earth. And is she really so remote from us? The contrary is true. Precisely because she is with God and in God, she is very close to each one of us. While she lived on this earth she could only be close to a few people. Being in God, who is close to us, actually, "within" all of us, Mary shares in this closeness of God. Being in God and with God, she is close to each one of us, knows our hearts, can hear our prayers, can help us with her motherly kindness and has been given to us, as the Lord said, precisely as a "mother" to whom we can turn at every moment. She always listens to us, she is always close to us, and being Mother of the Son, participates in the power of the Son and in his goodness. We can always entrust the whole of our lives to this Mother, who is not far from any one of us.

Homily on the Solemnity of the Assumption
August 15, 2005

84. *The things above*

Mary is an example and support for all believers: she encourages us not to lose confidence before the difficulties and inevitable problems of every day. She assures us of her help and reminds us that it is essential to seek and think of "the things above, not those of the earth" (cf. Col 3:2). Caught up in daily activities we risk, in fact, to think that here, in this world in which we are only passing through, is the ultimate goal of human existence. Instead, Paradise is the true goal of our earthly pilgrimage. How different our days would be if they were animated by this perspective! It was this way for the saints. Their lives witnessed to what they lived, with their hearts continually directed to God. Earthly realities are lived properly because the eternal truth of divine love illuminates them.

Homily on the Solemnity of the Assumption
August 15, 2006

85. *Gate of Heaven*

Heaven is our final dwelling place; from there, Mary encourages us by her example to welcome God's will, so as not to allow ourselves to be seduced by the deceptive attraction to what is transitory and fleeting, and not to give in to the temptations of selfishness and evil which extinguish the joy of life in the heart.

Homily on the Solemnity of the Assumption
August 15, 2005

86. *Mary and the Holy Spirit*

Full light is shed on the bond that united Mary with the Holy Spirit from the very beginning of her existence when, as she was being conceived, the Spirit, the eternal Love of the Father and of the Son, made their dwelling within her and preserved her from any shadow of sin; then again, when the same Spirit brought the Son of God into being in her womb; and yet again when, with the grace of the Spirit, Mary's own words were fulfilled through the whole span of her life: "Behold, I am the handmaid of the Lord"; and lastly, when, by the power of the Holy Spirit, Mary was taken up physically to be beside the Son in the glory of God the Father.

Address at the Shrine of Our Lady of Divine Love
May 1, 2006

IX. Marian
Devotion

87. *Homage to Mary*

In contemplating the face of Christ, and in Christ, the face of the Father, Mary Most Holy precedes, sustains and accompanies us. Love and devotion for the Mother of the Lord, so widespread and deeply rooted in the Italian People, are a precious heritage that we must always nurture and a great resource in view of evangelization.

> *Address to the fifty-fourth assembly of the*
> *Italian bishops' conference*
> *May 30, 2005*

88. *Church of Mary*

May the Virgin Mary, so loved and venerated in every part of Italy, precede and guide us in our union with Christ. In her we meet, pure and undeformed, the true essence of the Church, and so through her, we learn to know and love the mystery of the Church that lives in history, we deeply feel a part of it, and in our turn we become "ecclesial souls," we learn to resist that "internal secularization" that threatens the Church of our time, a consequence of the secularization process that has profoundly marked European civilization.

Address to the participants in the
Fourth National Ecclesial Convention of Italy
October 19, 2006

89. *Marian veneration*

True Marian devotion never obscures or diminishes faith and love for Jesus Christ Our Savior, the one Mediator between God and humankind. On the contrary, entrustment to Our Lady is a privileged path, tested by numerous saints, for a more faithful following of the Lord. Consequently, let us entrust ourselves to her with filial abandonment!

Address at the conclusion of the Marian month
May 31, 2006

90. *Mother most pure*

Looking at Mary, how can we, her children, fail to let the aspiration to beauty, goodness and purity of heart be aroused in us? Her heavenly candor draws us to God, helping us to overcome the temptation to live a mediocre life composed of compromises with evil, and directs us decisively towards the authentic good that is the source of joy.

Angelus
December 8, 2005

91. *Mother most admirable*

[All people] constantly experience the gift of [Mary's] goodness and the unfailing love which she pours out from the depths of her heart. The testimonials of gratitude, offered to her from every continent and culture, are a recognition of that pure love which is not self-seeking but simply benevolent. At the same time, the devotion of the faithful shows an infallible intuition of how such love is possible: it becomes so as a result of the most intimate union with God, through which the soul is totally pervaded by him—a condition which enables those who have drunk from the fountain of God's love to become in their turn a fountain from which "flow rivers of living water" (Jn 7:38). Mary, Virgin and Mother, shows us what love is and whence it draws its origin and its constantly renewed power. To her we entrust the Church and her mission in the service of love.

Encyclical letter God Is Love (Deus Caritas Est), *no. 42*
December 25, 2005

92. *Mother of consolation*

The closer a person is to God, the closer he [or she] is to people. We see this in Mary. The fact that she is totally with God is the reason why she is so close to human beings. For this reason she can be the Mother of every consolation and every help, a Mother whom anyone can dare to address in any kind of need in weakness and in sin, for she has understanding for everything and is for everyone the open power of creative goodness.

Homily on the fortieth anniversary of the
closing of the Second Vatican Council
December 8, 2005

93. *Our Lady of Lourdes*

We all know that the Virgin expressed God's tenderness for the suffering in the Grotto of Massabielle. This tenderness, this loving concern, is felt in an especially lively way in the world precisely on the day of the Feast of Our Lady of Lourdes, re-presenting in the liturgy, and especially in the Eucharist, the mystery of Christ, Redeemer of Man, of whom the Immaculate Virgin is the first fruit. In presenting herself to Bernadette as the Immaculate Conception, Mary Most Holy came to remind the modern world, which was in danger of forgetting it, of the primacy of divine grace which is stronger than sin and death.

Address to the sick at the end of Mass on the
Feast of Our Lady of Lourdes
February 11, 2006

94. *Our Lady of Mount Carmel*

The Carmelites have spread among the Christian people devotion to Our Lady of Mount Carmel, holding her up as a model of prayer, contemplation and dedication to God. Indeed, Mary was the first, in a way which can never be equaled, to believe and experience that Jesus, the Incarnate Word, is the summit, the peak of man's encounter with God. By fully accepting the Word, she "was blessedly brought to the holy Mountain" (cf. *Opening Prayer of the Memorial*), and lives for ever with the Lord in body and soul.

Angelus
July 16, 2006

95. *Seat of wisdom*

Learn from the Virgin Mary, the first person to contemplate the humanity of the Incarnate Word, the humanity of Divine Wisdom. In the Baby Jesus, with whom she had infinite and silent conversations, she recognized the human Face of God, so that the mysterious Wisdom of the Son was impressed on the Mother's mind and heart. So it was that Mary became the "Seat of Wisdom."

Address to teachers and students at Roman universities
December 14, 2006

96. *Queen of martyrs*

Mary, who held the Redeemer in her arms at Bethlehem, also suffers an interior martyrdom herself. She shared his passion and had to take him yet again in her arms when he was taken down from the Cross. To this Mother, who knew the joy of his birth and the torment of the death of her divine Son, we entrust all those who are persecuted and suffering in various ways for their witness and service to the Gospel.

Angelus
December 26, 2006

97. *Queen of the most holy Rosary*

[We celebrate] the feast of Our Lady of the Rosary, and it is as though Our Lady invites us every year to rediscover the beauty of this prayer, so simple and so profound.

Angelus
October 1, 2006

98. Queen of the family

[Mary is] the Mother who protects by her love God's family on its earthly pilgrimage. Mary is the image and model of all mothers, of their great mission to be guardians of life, of their mission to be teachers of the art of living and of the art of loving.

Homily at Mass for the Fifth World Meeting of Families
July 9, 2006

99. Queen of the Church

The icon of the Annunciation, more than any other, helps us to see clearly how everything in the Church goes back to that mystery of Mary's acceptance of the divine Word, by which, through the action of the Holy Spirit, the Covenant between God and humanity was perfectly sealed. Everything in the Church, every institution and ministry, including that of Peter and his Successors, is "included" under the Virgin's mantle, within the grace-filled horizon of her "yes" to God's will.

Homily at the consistory for the creation of new cardinals
March 25, 2006

100. *Personal praise of Mary*

I would . . . like to express to Mary my gratitude for the support she offers me in my daily service to the Church. I know that I can count on her help in every situation; indeed, I know that she foresees with maternal intuition all her children's needs and intervenes effectively to sustain them: this has been the experience of the Christian people ever since its first steps in Jerusalem.

Address at the conclusion of the Marian month
May 31, 2006

X. Prayers
to Mary

Prayer to Mary (I)

Yes, we want to thank you, Virgin Mother of God and our most beloved Mother, for your intercession for the good of the Church. You, who in embracing the divine will without reserve were consecrated with all of your energies to the person and work of your Son, teach us to keep in our heart and to meditate in silence, as you did, upon the mysteries of Christ's life.

May you who reached Calvary, ever-deeply united to your Son who from the Cross gave you as mother to the disciple John, also make us feel you are always close in each moment of our lives, especially in times of darkness and trial.

You, who at Pentecost, together with the Apostles in prayer, called upon the gift of the Holy Spirit for the new-born Church, help us to persevere in the faithful following of Christ. To you, a "sign of certain hope and comfort," we trustfully turn our gaze "until the day of the Lord shall come" (*Lumen Gentium*, no. 68).

You, Mary, are invoked with the insistent prayer of the faithful throughout the world so that you, exalted above all the angels and saints, will intercede before your Son for us, "until all families of peoples, whether they are honored with the title of Christian or whether they still do not know the Savior, may be happily gathered together in peace and harmony into one People of God, for the glory of the Most Holy and Undivided Trinity" (*Lumen Gentium*, no. 69). Amen.

Prayer on the Feast of the Immaculate Conception
December 8, 2005

Prayer to Mary (II)

Holy Mary, Mother of God,
you have given the world its true light,
Jesus, your Son—the Son of God.
You abandoned yourself completely
to God's call
and thus became a wellspring
of the goodness which flows forth from him.
Show us Jesus. Lead us to him.
Teach us to know and love him,
so that we too can become
capable of true love
and be fountains of living water
in the midst of a thirsting world.

Encyclical letter God Is Love (Deus Caritas Est)*, no. 42*
December 25, 2005

Prayer to Mary (III)

Your Son, just before his farewell to his disciples, said to them: "Whoever wishes to become great among you must be your servant, and whoever wishes to be first among you must be slave of all" (Mk 10:43-44). At the decisive hour in your own life, you said: "Here I am, the servant of the Lord" (Lk 1:38). You lived your whole life as service. And you continue to do so throughout history. At Cana, you silently and discreetly interceded for the spouses, and so you continue to do. You take upon yourself people's needs and concerns, and you bring them before the Lord, before your Son. Your power is goodness. Your power is service.

Teach us—great and small alike—to carry out our responsibilities in the same way. Help us to find the strength to offer reconciliation and forgiveness. Help us to become patient and humble, but also free and courageous, just as you were at the hour of the Cross. In your arms you hold Jesus, the Child who blesses, the Child who is also the Lord of the world. By holding the Child who blesses, you have yourself become a blessing. Bless us, this city and this country! Show us Jesus, the blessed fruit of your womb! Pray for us sinners, now and at the hour of our death. Amen!

Prayer at the Marian shrine of Munchen, Germany
September 9, 2006

Prayer to Mary (IV)

"*Full of grace*" are you, Mary, full of divine love from the very first moment of your existence, providentially predestined to be Mother of the Redeemer and intimately connected to him in the mystery of salvation. In your Immaculate Conception shines forth the vocation of Christ's disciples, called to become, with his grace, saints and immaculate through love (cf. Eph 1:4). In you shines the dignity of every human being who is always precious in the Creator's eyes. Those who look to you, All Holy Mother, never lose their serenity, no matter what the hardships of life. Although the experience of sin is a sad one since it disfigures the dignity of God's children, anyone who turns to you discovers the beauty of truth and love and finds the path that leads to the Father's house.

"*Full of grace*" are you, Mary, which, welcoming with your "yes" to the Creator's plan, opened to us the path of salvation. Teach us also at your school to say our "yes" to the Lord's will. Let it be a "yes" that joins with your own "yes," without reservations or shadows, a "yes" that the Heavenly Father willed to have need of in order to beget the new Man, Christ, the one Savior of the world and of history. Give us the courage to say "no" to the deceptions of power, money, pleasure; to dishonest earnings, corruption and hypocrisy, to selfishness and violence; "no" to the Evil One, the deceitful prince of this world; to say "yes" to Christ, who destroys the power of evil with the omnipotence of love. We know that only hearts converted to Love, which is God, can build a better future for all.

"Full of grace" are you, Mary! For all generations your name is a pledge of sure hope. Yes! Because as the great poet, Dante, wrote, for us mortals you are "a source of living hope" (*Paradiso*, XXXIII, 12). Let us come once again as trusting pilgrims to draw faith and comfort, joy and love, safety and peace from this source, the wellspring of your Immaculate Heart.

Virgin "full of grace," show yourself to be a tender and caring Mother to those who live in this city of yours, so that the true Gospel spirit may enliven and guide their conduct; show yourself as Mother and watchful keeper of Italy and Europe, so that people may draw from their ancient Christian roots fresh vigor to build their present and their future; show yourself as a provident and merciful Mother to the whole world so that, by respecting human dignity and rejecting every form of violence and exploitation, sound foundations may be laid for the civilization of love. Show yourself as Mother, especially to those most in need: the defenseless, the marginalized and outcasts, to the victims of a society that all too often sacrifices the human person for other ends and interests.

Show yourself, O Mary, as Mother of all, and give us Christ, the Hope of the world! "*Monstra Te esse Matrem*," O Virgin Immaculate, full of grace! Amen!

Prayer on the Feast of the Immaculate Conception
December 8, 2006

Prayer to Mary (V)

Let us entrust to Mary, who is the Mother of Mercy incarnate, particularly those situations to which the Lord's grace alone can bring peace, comfort and justice.

The Virgin heard the Angel announcing her divine Motherhood say to her: "With God nothing will be impossible" (Lk 1:37). Mary believed and for this reason she is blessed (cf. Lk 1:45). What is impossible to man becomes possible to the one who believes (cf. Mk 9:23).

Thus . . . let us ask the Mother of God to obtain for us the gift of a mature faith: a faith that we would like to resemble hers as far as possible, a clear, genuine, humble and at the same time courageous faith, steeped in hope and enthusiasm for the Kingdom of God, a faith devoid of all fatalism and wholly set on cooperating with the divine will in full and joyful obedience and with the absolute certainty that God wants nothing but love and life, always and for everyone.

Obtain for us, O Mary, an authentic, pure faith. May you always be thanked and blessed, Holy Mother of God! Amen!

Homily at First Vespers, Solemnity of Mary,
Mother of God
December 31, 2006

VOLUME TWO

t the school of Mary we can understand with our hearts what our eyes and minds do not manage to perceive or contain on their own.

Pope Benedict XVI

PREFACE

ntroducing the story of the wedding in Cana, the gospel writer John recounts: "On the third day there was a wedding in Cana in Galilee, and the mother of Jesus was there. Jesus and his disciples were also invited to the wedding" (Jn 2:1-2).

Mary was present alongside Jesus! And she was present with her maternal sensibility, capable of intuiting the uneasiness of the spouses and of translating it into courageous prayer.

At the end of the story, John observes: "Jesus did this as the beginning of his signs in Cana in Galilee and so revealed his glory, and his disciples began to believe in him" (Jn 2:11).

Mary—this detail is so wonderful!—causes the first spark of faith in the hearts of the disciples. Is it not legitimate to imagine that the Apostles often spoke of her? Is it not legitimate to imagine that they asked her about the birth of Jesus and the early years of his life? Is it not legitimate to imagine that at the time of the Passion, the Apostles ran to Mary to seek a light of hope and a flash of the Resurrection in her eyes? Is it not legitimate to imagine that Mary, at sunset one evening, confided to the Apostles her excitement during the Annunciation and the joy that she felt after having stated her "yes"?

The Holy Father Benedict XVI loves calling Mary *the woman of the "yes"* and writes: "Meditating on the Immaculate Conception of Mary is therefore allowing oneself to be drawn by the 'yes' that marvelously joined her to the mission of Christ, the redeemer of humanity." And he adds: "Turn your eyes to the Virgin Mary, and learn from her 'yes' to pronounce your own 'yes' to the divine call as well."

These pages collect many of the beautiful tesserae composing the extraordinary mosaic that is Benedict XVI's Marian devotion. It is my hope that this selection of thoughts, as fresh as a springtime field, will be approached by many readers so that every once in a while they can pick a flower and take in its delicate scent. They will certainly draw comfort and encouragement from it on their journey.

Cardinal Angelo Comastri
Vicar General of His Holiness for the
State of Vatican City

Introduction

his second volume of Marian thoughts, a year after the first, shows the Holy Father's constant and prolific attention to the person of Mary. References to the Holy Mother of the Redeemer are very frequent in Pope Benedict XVI's homilies, speeches, and general statements. She is in fact the spiritual model who helps guide any existence, starting with that first "yes" built on docility and self-abandonment to the will of God, which made real and tangible his "entering this world and its history" (*On Christian Hope* [*Spe Salvi*], no. 50).

Using a rapid approach that seeks only the essential without delay, these thoughts touch upon the entire life of Our Lady starting with the Visitation, that journey of joy in which Pope Benedict sees a prefiguration "of the Church to come, which carries the hope of the world in her womb across the mountains of history" (*On Christian Hope* [*Spe Salvi*], no. 50). The life of Mary then unfolds through scenes in which the conflict between light and shadow is always apparent. In Bethlehem, the contrast between the Angels' announcement and the material poverty in which God is sheltered and welcomed is jarring, and is replete with analogies to our present, in which man is so busy and concerned with "his own things, that nothing remains for others—for his neighbor, for the poor, for God" (Homily, December 25, 2007). Together with the announcement of salvation and illumination, Mary learned of the contradiction and the Cross from wise Simeon on the feast of the Presentation of Jesus at the temple. Then, in following Jesus during the years of his public life, she saw the atmosphere "of hostility and rejection" that was building up around Jesus become increasingly tangible up to the hour of the Cross, the hour of suffering that would end up making Mary not only the Mother of God but "the mother of all those who believe in your Son Jesus and wish to follow him" (*On Christian Hope* [*Spe Salvi*], no. 50). Indeed, at the foot of the Cross the Lord gave Mary to the disciple whom he loved and, in him, to all of us. It is the beginning of a new journey, a journey of believers who entrust themselves to her in their needs and hopes, in their joys and sufferings, and a journey which would bring those same disciples who fled during persecution to draw together in prayer around her in awaiting the Holy Spirit, forming "an icon of the nascent Church [that] should be a constant source of inspiration for every Christian community" (Message, July 20, 2007).

Within this biographical and narrative plot, Pope Benedict constantly identifies important consequences for the lives of all. As is often repeated in these selected thoughts, Mary is the mother of the "yes." She is the model for those who believe, for those who trust in God. In fact, Mary is she who can bring forth Christ because she first believed. She embodies the faith ideal that the Holy Father has been repeating to all since being elected pope: one cannot see Christ without believing in him (cf. General Audience, April 19, 2006). Pope Benedict again reminds us that with her "yes," Mary points in her person to an essential dimension of human beings: "their capacity for openness to God and his word of truth" (Speech, September 7, 2007). The Holy Father continually invites us to imitate Mary and to welcome this Word so that "by the power of the Holy Spirit, Christ may once again take flesh in the 'today' of our history" (Homily, May 13, 2007), and so that we can reciprocally offer the world a Gospel like hers, which "did not communicate to the world an idea but Jesus, the Incarnate Word" (Angelus, December 23, 2007).

These are just some small hints of a much richer and more complex interlacement of topics that can be discovered in Pope Benedict's spiritual interpretation of the figure of Our Lady. With this book, he gives us the possibility of personally continuing his meditations and extending them into our lives so that the model of sanctity and beauty embodied by the Holy Virgin can touch our own existence and transform it, because we have also been made capable of proclaiming the greatness of the Lord together with the spirit and soul of Mary, and of bringing Christ into our world again today (cf. Angelus, September 9, 2007).

Edmund Caruana, OCarm

1. *Act of entrustment to Mary*

Let us entrust ourselves to her so that she may guide our steps in this new period of time which the Lord gives us to live, and help us to be authentic friends of his Son and thus also courageous builders of his Kingdom in the world, a Kingdom of light and truth.

General Audience
January 2, 2008

I. THE LISTENING VIRGIN

2. *Listening*

From the Annunciation to Pentecost, Mary of Nazareth appears as someone whose freedom is completely open to God's will. Her immaculate conception is revealed precisely in her unconditional docility to God's word. Obedient faith in response to God's work shapes her life at every moment. A virgin attentive to God's word, she lives in complete harmony with his will; she treasures in her heart the words that come to her from God and, piecing them together like a mosaic, she learns to understand them more deeply (cf. Lk 2:19, 51); Mary is the great Believer who places herself confidently in God's hands, abandoning herself to his will. This mystery deepens as she becomes completely involved in the redemptive mission of Jesus.

Apostolic Exhortation The Sacrament of Charity
(Sacramentum Caritatis), *no. 33*
February 22, 2007

3. *At a school of prayer*

Mary shows us the way. St. Luke says twice that the Virgin Mary "kept all these things, pondering them in her heart" (2:19; cf. 2:51). She was a person in conversation with God, with the Word of God and also with the events through which God spoke to her. The *Magnificat* is a "fabric" woven of words from Sacred Scripture. It shows us how Mary lived in a permanent conversation with the Word of God, and thus, with God himself. Then of course, in life with the Lord, she was also always in conversation with Christ, with the Son of God and with the Trinitarian God. Therefore, let us learn from Mary and speak personally with the Lord, pondering and preserving God's words in our lives and hearts so that they may become true food for each one of us. Thus, Mary guides us at a school of prayer in personal and profound contact with God.

Lenten meeting with the clergy of Rome
February 22, 2007

4. *Openness*

The person of Mary reminds us of an essential dimension of human beings: their capacity for openness to God and his word of truth.

Address at the welcome ceremony in Austria
September 7, 2007

II. MOTHER OF THE "YES"

5. *Conceived without sin*

The mystery of God's grace . . . enfolded her from the first instant of her existence as the creature destined to be Mother of the Redeemer, preserving her from the stain of original sin. Looking at her, we recognize the loftiness and beauty of God's plan for everyone: to become holy and immaculate in love (cf. Eph 1:4), in the image of our Creator.

Angelus
December 8, 2007

6. *The icon of the Immaculate Conception*

For this reason, Mary is a model of total self-abandonment to God's will: she received in her heart the eternal Word and she conceived it in her virginal womb; she trusted in God and, with her soul pierced by a sword (cf. Lk 2:35), she did not hesitate to share the Passion of her Son, renewing on Calvary at the foot of the Cross her "yes" of the Annunciation. To reflect upon the Immaculate Conception of Mary is thus to allow oneself to be attracted by the "yes" which joined her wonderfully to the mission of Christ, Redeemer of humanity; it is to allow oneself to be taken and led by her hand to pronounce in one's turn "*fiat*" to the will of God, with all one's existence interwoven with joys and sadness, hopes and disappointments, in the awareness that tribulations, pain and suffering make rich the meaning of our pilgrimage on the earth.

Message for the Sixteenth World Day of the Sick
January 11, 2008

7. *Call*

Direct your gaze to the Virgin Mary and from her "yes," learn also to pronounce your "yes" to the divine call. The Holy Spirit enters into our lives in the measure in which we open our hearts with our "yes": the fuller the "yes," the fuller is the gift of his presence.

Meeting with university students of Rome
December 13, 2007

8. *Full of grace*

Mary is greeted by the Angel as "full of grace," which means exactly this: her heart and her life are totally open to God, and this is why she is completely pervaded by his grace. May she help you to make yourselves a free and full "yes" to God, so that you can be renewed, indeed, transformed by the light and joy of the Holy Spirit.

Meeting with university students of Rome
December 13, 2007

9. *Invitation*

Mary [is the] Mother of the Good Shepherd. May she who responded promptly to God's call, saying: "Behold, I am the handmaid of the Lord" (Lk 1:38), help all of us to accept with joy and willingness Christ's invitation to be his disciples, always motivated to be "of one heart and soul" (cf. Acts 4:32).

Regina Caeli
April 29, 2007

10. God's "yes"

Let us look above all at Mary. At her school, we too, like her, can experience that "yes" of God to humanity from which flow all the "yeses" of our life.

Homily at Mass in Loreto, Italy
September 2, 2007

III. THE MOTHERHOOD OF MARY

11. *Immense gift*

At Bethlehem, in the fullness of time, Jesus was born of Mary; the Son of God was made man for our salvation, and the Virgin became the true Mother of God. This immense gift that Mary has received is not reserved to her alone, but is for us all. In her fruitful virginity, in fact, God has given "to men the goods of eternal salvation . . . because by means of her we have received the Author of Life" (cf. *Collect Prayer*). Mary, therefore, after having given flesh to the Only-Begotten Son of God, became the mother of believers and of all humanity.

Angelus
January 1, 2008

12. *Great light*

This is Christmas—the historical event and the mystery of love, which for more than two thousand years has spoken to men and women of every era and every place. It is the holy day on which the "great light" of Christ shines forth, bearing peace! Certainly, if we are to recognize it, if we are to receive it, faith is needed and humility is needed. The humility of Mary, who believed in the word of the Lord and, bending low over the manger, was the first to adore the fruit of her womb.

Urbi et Orbi *message for Christmas*
December 25, 2007

13. *In swaddling clothes*

"The time came for Mary to be delivered. And she gave birth to her first-born son and wrapped him in swaddling clothes, and laid him in a manger, because there was no room for them in the inn" (Lk 2:6-7). These words touch our hearts every time we hear them. This was the moment that the angel had foretold at Nazareth: "you will bear a son, and you shall call his name Jesus. He will be great, and will be called the Son of the Most High" (Lk 1:31). This was the moment that Israel had been awaiting for centuries, through many dark hours—the moment that all mankind was somehow awaiting, in terms as yet ill-defined: when God would take care of us, when he would step outside his concealment, when the world would be saved and God would renew all things. We can imagine the kind of interior preparation, the kind of love with which Mary approached that hour. The brief phrase "She wrapped him in swaddling clothes" allows us to glimpse something of the holy joy and the silent zeal of that preparation. The swaddling clothes were ready, so that the child could be given a fitting welcome. Yet there is no room at the inn. In some way, mankind is awaiting God, waiting for him to draw near. But when the moment comes, there is no room for him. Man is so preoccupied with himself, he has such urgent need of all the space and all the time for his own things, that nothing remains for others—for his neighbor, for the poor, for God. And the richer men become, the more they fill up all the space by themselves. And the less room there is for others.

Homily at Midnight Mass, Solemnity of the
Nativity of the Lord
December 25, 2007

14. *Our mother*

"When the time had fully come," [St. Paul] wrote, "God sent forth his Son, born of woman" (Gal 4:4). The Church contemplates in the "woman" the features of Mary of Nazareth, a unique woman because she was called to carry out a mission that brought her into very close contact with Christ: indeed, it was an absolutely unique relationship, because Mary is Mother of the Savior. Just as obviously, however, we can and must affirm that she is our Mother because, by living her very special maternal relationship with the Son, she shared in his mission *for us* and *for the salvation of all people*. In contemplating her, the Church makes out her own features: Mary lives faith and charity; Mary is also a creature saved by the one Savior; Mary collaborates in the initiative of the salvation of all humanity. Thus, Mary constitutes for the Church her truest image: she in whom the Ecclesial Community must continually discover the authentic sense of its own vocation and its own mystery.

Homily at First Vespers, Solemnity of Mary,
Mother of God
December 31, 2007

15. *The solicitude of Mary*

[Mary is] a completely singular mother, for she was chosen in advance by God for a unique and mysterious mission: to bring forth to earthly life the Father's Eternal Word, who came into the world for the salvation of all people. And Mary, Immaculate in her conception . . . traveled her earthly pilgrimage sustained by undaunted faith, steadfast hope and humble and boundless love, following in the footsteps of her Son, Jesus. She was close to him with motherly solicitude from his birth to Calvary, where she witnessed his crucifixion, transfixed by suffering but with unwavering hope. She then experienced the joy of the Resurrection, at dawn on the third day, the new day, when the Crucified One left the tomb, overcoming for ever and definitively the power of sin and death.

Prayer at the Spanish Steps for the
Feast of the Immaculate Conception
December 8, 2007

16. *Mother of the Redeemer*

Thus, the description "Mother of God," so deeply bound up with the Christmas festivities, is therefore the fundamental name with which the Community of Believers has always honored the Blessed Virgin. It clearly explains Mary's mission in salvation history. All other titles attributed to Our

Lady are based on her vocation to be the Mother of the Redeemer, the human creature chosen by God to bring about the plan of salvation, centered on the great mystery of the Incarnation of the Divine Word.

General Audience
January 2, 2008

17. *The mystery of the Incarnation*

The Evangelist Luke repeats several times that Our Lady meditated silently on these extraordinary events in which God had involved her. We also heard this in the short Gospel passage that the Liturgy presents to us today. "Mary kept all these things, pondering them in her heart" (Lk 2:19). The Greek verb used, *sumbállousa*, literally means "piecing together" and makes us think of a great mystery to be discovered little by little. Although the Child lying in a manger looks like all children in the world, at the same time he is totally different: he is the Son of God, he is God, true God and true man. This mystery—the Incarnation of the Word and the divine Motherhood of Mary—is great and certainly far from easy to understand with the human mind alone.

Homily on the Solemnity of Mary, Mother of God
January 1, 2008

18. *Twofold motherhood*

[Mary] is mother because she brought forth Jesus in the flesh; she is mother because she adhered totally to the Father's will. St. Augustine wrote: "The divine motherhood would have been of no value to her had Christ not borne her in his heart, with a destiny more fortunate than the moment when she conceived him in the flesh" (*De Sancta Virginitate*, 3, 3).

Homily on the Solemnity of Mary, Mother of God
January 1, 2008

IV. Woman of Faith

19. *The faith of Mary*

The Virgin Mary . . . with her faith and maternal labors collaborated in a unique way in our Redemption to the point that Elizabeth proclaimed her "Blessed . . . among women" (Lk 1:42), adding: "Blessed is she who believed . . ." (Lk 1:45). Having become a disciple of her Son, Mary manifested total trust in him at Cana (cf. Jn 2:5), and followed him to the foot of the Cross where she received from him a maternal mission for all his disciples of all times, represented by John [cf. Jn 19:25-27].

General Audience
February 14, 2007

20. *School of faith*

Mary Most Holy, the pure and immaculate Virgin, is for us a school of faith destined to guide us and give us strength on the path that leads us to the Creator of Heaven and Earth. . . . Take inspiration from her teachings, seek to welcome and to preserve in your hearts the enlightenment that she, by divine mandate, sends you from on high.

> *Meeting with priests, seminarians, deacons,*
> *and men and women religious in Brazil*
> *May 12, 2007*

21. *"Nothing will be impossible for God" (Lk 1:37)*

Nothing is impossible for those who trust in God and entrust themselves to him. Look at the young Mary; the Angel proposed something truly inconceivable to her: participation, in the most involving way possible, in the greatest of God's plans, the salvation of humanity. Facing this proposal, Mary, as we heard in the Gospel, was distressed for she realized the smallness of her being before the omnipotence of God; and she asked herself: "How is it possible? Why should it be me?" Yet, ready to do the divine will, she promptly said her "yes" which changed her life and the history of all humanity.

> *Prayer vigil with young people in Loreto, Italy*
> *September 1, 2007*

22. *Without reservations*

The love of God, who surrendered himself into our hands for our salvation, gives us the inner freedom to let go of our own lives, in order to find true life. Mary's participation in this love gave her the strength to say "yes" unconditionally. In her encounter with the gentle, respectful love of God, who awaits the free cooperation of his creature in order to bring about his saving plan, the Blessed Virgin was able to overcome all hesitation and, in view of this great and unprecedented plan, to entrust herself into his hands. With complete availability, interior openness and freedom, she allowed God to fill her with love, with his Holy Spirit. Mary, the simple woman, could thus receive within herself the Son of God, and give to the world the Savior who had first given himself to her.

Angelus
September 9, 2007

23. *Mother of Trust*

Mary, Mother of Trust! This most pacifying title corresponds to the invitation, repeated in the Gospel and addressed to the Virgin by the Angel and then so many other times by Jesus to his disciples: "Do not be afraid" (cf. Lk 1:30). "Do not be afraid, for I am with you," says the Lord. In the icon of Our Lady of Trust, in which the Child points to the Mother, it seems that Jesus is adding, "Look at your Mother and do not fear."

Homily at First Vespers, Feast of Our Lady of Trust
February 1, 2008

V. Woman of Hope

24. *Star of the Sea*

With a hymn composed in the eighth or ninth century, thus for over a thousand years, the Church has greeted Mary, the Mother of God, as "Star of the Sea": *Ave maris stella*. Human life is a journey. Towards what destination? How do we find the way? Life is like a voyage on the sea of history, often dark and stormy, a voyage in which we watch for the stars that indicate the route. The true stars of our life are the people who have lived good lives. They are lights of hope. Certainly, Jesus Christ is the true light, the sun that has risen above all the shadows of history. But to reach him we also need lights close by—people who shine with his light and so guide us along our way. Who more than Mary could be a star of hope for us? With her "yes" she opened the door of our world to God himself; she became the living Ark of the Covenant, in whom God took flesh, became one of us, and pitched his tent among us (cf. Jn 1:14).

Encyclical letter Spe Salvi (On Christian Hope), *no. 49*
November 30, 2007

25. *Mother of Hope*

Holy Mary, you belonged to the humble and great souls of Israel who, like Simeon, were "looking for the consolation of Israel" (Lk 2:25) and hoping, like Anna, "for the redemption of Jerusalem" (Lk 2:38). Your life was thoroughly imbued with the sacred scriptures of Israel which spoke of hope, of the promise made to Abraham and his descendants (cf. Lk 1:55). In this way we can appreciate the holy fear that overcame you when the angel of the Lord appeared to you and told you that you would give birth to the One who was the hope of Israel, the One awaited by the world. Through you, through your "yes," the hope of the ages became reality, entering this world and its history. You bowed low before the greatness of this task and gave your consent: "Behold, I am the handmaid of the Lord; let it be to me according to your word" (Lk 1:38). When you hastened with holy joy across the mountains of Judea to see your cousin Elizabeth, you became the image of the Church to come, which carries the hope of the world in her womb across the mountains of history. But alongside the joy which, with your *Magnificat*, you proclaimed in word and song for all the centuries to hear, you also knew the dark sayings of the prophets about the suffering of the servant of God in this world. Shining over his birth in the stable at Bethlehem, there were angels in splendor who brought the good news to the shepherds, but at the same time the lowliness of God in this world was all too palpable. The old man Simeon spoke to you of the sword which would pierce your soul (cf. Lk 2:35), of the sign of contradiction that your Son would be in this world. Then, when Jesus began his public ministry, you had to step aside, so that a new family could grow, the family which it was his mission to establish and which would be made up of those who heard his word and kept it (cf. Lk 11:27ff.). Notwithstanding the great joy that marked the beginning of Jesus' ministry, in the synagogue of Nazareth you must already have experienced the truth of the saying about the "sign of contradiction" (cf. Lk 4:28ff.). In this way you saw the growing power of hostility and rejection which built up around Jesus until the hour of the Cross, when you had to look upon the Savior of the world, the heir of David, the Son of God dying like a failure, exposed to mockery, between criminals. Then you received the word of Jesus: "Woman, behold, your Son!" (Jn 19:26). From the Cross you received a new mission. From the Cross you became a mother in a new way: the mother of all those who believe in your Son Jesus and wish to follow him. The sword of sorrow pierced your heart. Did hope die? Did the world remain definitively without light, and life without purpose? At that moment, deep down, you probably listened again to the word spoken by the angel in answer to your fear at the time of the Annunciation: "Do not be afraid, Mary!" (Lk 1:30). How many times had the Lord, your Son, said the same thing to his disciples: do not be afraid! In your heart, you heard this word again during the night of Golgotha. Before the hour of his betrayal he had said to his disciples: "Be of good cheer, I have overcome the world" (Jn 16:33). "Let not your hearts be troubled, neither let them be afraid" (Jn 14:27). "Do not be afraid, Mary!" In that hour at Nazareth the angel had also said to you: "Of his kingdom there will be no end" (Lk 1:33). Could it have ended before it began? No, at the foot of the Cross, on the strength of Jesus' own word, you became the mother of believers. In this faith, which even in the darkness of Holy Saturday bore the certitude of hope, you made your way towards Easter morning. The joy of the Resurrection touched your heart and united you in a new way to the disciples, destined to become the family of Jesus through faith. In this way you were in the midst of the community of believers, who in the days following the Ascension prayed with one voice for the gift of the Holy Spirit (cf. Acts 1:14) and then received that gift on the day of Pentecost. The "Kingdom" of Jesus was not as might have been imagined. It began in that hour, and of this "Kingdom" there will be no end. Thus you remain in the midst of the disciples as their Mother, as the Mother of hope. Holy Mary, Mother of God, our Mother, teach us to believe, to hope, to love with you. Show us the way to his Kingdom! Star of the Sea, shine upon us and guide us on our way!

Encyclical letter Spe Salvi (On Christian Hope), *no. 50*
November 30, 2007

26. *Star of Hope*

Who could be a better "Star of Hope" for us than Mary? With her "yes," with the generous offering of freedom received from the Creator, she enabled the hope of the millennia to become reality, to enter this world and its history. Through her God took flesh, became one of us and pitched his tent among us.

Prayer at the Spanish Steps for the
Feast of the Immaculate Conception
December 8, 2007

VI. WOMAN OF CHARITY

27. *Along the way of charity*

What drove Mary, a young woman, to undertake that journey [to Elizabeth]? What, above all, led her to forget herself, to spend the first three months of her pregnancy at the service of her cousin in need of help? The response is written in a Psalm: "I will run in the way of your commands when you enlarged my understanding" (Ps 119[118]: 32). The Holy Spirit, who makes the Son of God present in Mary's flesh, enlarged her heart to God's dimensions and urged her along the way of charity.

> *Address at the conclusion of the Marian month*
> *May 31, 2007*

28. *The Visitation*

The Visitation of Mary is understood in light of the event that immediately preceded it in Luke's account in the Gospel: the Annunciation of the Angel and the conception of Jesus by the work of the Holy Spirit. The Spirit descended upon the Virgin, the power of the Most High overshadowed her (cf. Lk 1:35). That same Spirit impelled her to "rise" and depart without hesitation (cf. Lk 1:39) in order to help her aged relative. Jesus had just begun to form himself in the womb of Mary, but his Spirit had already filled her heart so that the Mother was already beginning to follow her divine Son. On the way that leads from Galilee to Judea it was Jesus himself who "urged" Mary on, instilling in her a generous desire to go to the aid of her neighbor in need, the courage not to put her own legitimate needs, difficulties, worries, the dangers to her own life first. It is Jesus who helped her to overcome everything, allowing her to be guided by faith that works through charity (cf. Gal 5:6).

Address at the conclusion of the Marian month
May 31, 2007

29. *The heart of Mary*

The heart of Mary is visited by the grace of the Father, is permeated by the power of the Spirit and interiorly compelled by the Son; that is, we see a perfectly human heart inserted into the dynamism of the Most Holy Trinity. This movement is charity, which is perfect in Mary and becomes the model of the Church's charity, a manifestation of Trinitarian love (cf. Pope Benedict XVI, *Deus Caritas Est*, no. 19). Every gesture of genuine love, even the smallest, contains within it a spark of the infinite mystery of God.

Address at the conclusion of the Marian month
May 31, 2007

30. *Generosity*

May the Virgin Mary help us to make the most of the present time to listen to and put into practice [the] words of God. May she obtain for us that we become more attentive to our brethren in need, to share with them the much or the little that we have and to contribute, starting with ourselves, to spreading the logic and style of authentic solidarity.

Angelus
September 30, 2007

31. *Gift*

May the Virgin Mary, who offered the whole of herself to the Almighty and was filled with every Grace and Blessing with the coming of the Son of God, teach us to make our existence a daily gift to God the Father at the service of our brethren as we listen to his Word and his will.

Visit to the "Gift of Mary" House of the
Missionaries of Charity in the Vatican
January 4, 2008

VII. Mother of Sorrows

32. *Mother of Sorrows*

Mary, who with her faith accompanied her Son beneath the Cross, she who by a mysterious plan was associated to the sufferings of Christ her Son, never tires to exhort us to live and share with serene trust the experience of sorrow and sickness, offering it with faith to the Father, thus completing in our flesh what is lacking in the sufferings of Christ (cf. Col 1:24).

> *Address to the sick at the end of Mass on the*
> *Feast of Our Lady of Lourdes*
> *February 11, 2007*

33. *Faithful Virgin*

Our Lady . . . on Calvary sealed the "yes" she pronounced at Nazareth. United to Christ, Witness of the Father's love, Mary lived martyrdom of the soul.

> *Angelus*
> *March 25, 2007*

34. *At the foot of the Cross*

[The Cross of Christ] is the tree of life! At its foot you will always find Mary, Mother of Jesus. With her, Seat of Wisdom, turn your gaze to the One who was pierced for our sake (cf. Jn 19:37), contemplate the inexhaustible source of love and truth, and you too will be able to become joyful disciples and witnesses.

Address after praying the Rosary with university students
March 10, 2007

35. *Guide*

Let us ask the Virgin Mary, pierced in spirit next to the Cross of her Son, to obtain for us a solid faith. Guiding us along the Lenten journey, may she help us to leave all that distances us from listening to Christ and his saving Word.

Angelus
February 25, 2007

36. *Following Jesus*

From the Annunciation to the Cross, Mary is the one who received the Word, made flesh within her and then silenced in death. It is she, lastly, who took into her arms the lifeless body of the one who truly loved his own "to the end" (Jn 13:1).

> *Apostolic Exhortation* The Sacrament of Charity
> (Sacramentum Caritatis), *no. 33*
> *February 22, 2007*

37. *The Sorrowful Virgin*

The Virgin Mary, whom today's liturgy presents to us for contemplation at the foot of the Cross, [is] closely associated in Christ's mission and, as the Sorrowful Mother, a sharer in the work of salvation. On Calvary, Jesus gave her to us as Mother and entrusted us to her as children. May the Sorrowful Virgin obtain for you the gift of following her divine Crucified Son and of embracing serenely the difficulties and trials of daily life.

> *Meeting with the Poor Clares of Immaculate*
> *Conception Convent, Albano Laziale, Rome*
> *September 15, 2007*

38. *Our Lady of Holy Saturday*

Holy Saturday is the day when the liturgy is hushed, the day of great silence, and Christians are invited to preserve interior recollection, often difficult to encourage in our day, in order to be better prepared for the *Easter Vigil*. Spiritual retreats and Marian prayer meetings are organized in many communities in order to be united with the Mother of the Redeemer, who waited, anxious but trusting, for the Resurrection of her Crucified Son.

General Audience
April 4, 2007

39. *Suffering together*

Associated with the Sacrifice of Christ, Mary, *Mater Dolorosa*, who at the foot of the Cross suffers with her divine Son, is felt to be especially near by the Christian community, which gathers around its suffering members who bear the signs of the passion of the Lord. Mary suffers with those who are in affliction, with them she hopes, and she is their comfort, supporting them with her maternal help.

Message for the Sixteenth World Day of the Sick
January 11, 2008

VIII. Virgin of the Upper Room

40. *Pentecost*

The first Pentecost took place when Mary Most Holy was present amid the disciples in the Upper Room in Jerusalem and prayed. Today, too, let us entrust ourselves to her maternal intercession, so that the Holy Spirit may descend in abundance upon the Church in our day, fill the hearts of all the faithful and enkindle in them[, in us,] the fire of his love.

Regina Caeli
May 27, 2007

41. *Praying with Mary*

If we are to understand the mission of the Church, we must go back to the Upper Room where the disciples remained together (cf. Lk 24:49), praying with Mary, the "Mother," awaiting the Spirit that had been promised. This icon of the nascent Church should be a constant source of inspiration for every Christian community. Apostolic and missionary fruitfulness is not principally due to programs and pastoral methods that are cleverly drawn up and "efficient," but is the result of the community's constant prayer (cf. Pope Paul VI, *Evangelii Nuntiandi*, no. 75).

> *Message for the Twenty-Third World Youth Day*
> *July 20, 2007*

42. *Renewal*

Where Mary is, there is the archetype of total self-giving and Christian discipleship. Where Mary is, there is the pentecostal breath of the Holy Spirit; there is new beginning and authentic renewal.

> *Address at Heiligenkreuz Abbey, Austria*
> *September 9, 2007*

IX. Queen Assumed into Heaven

43. *Iconography of Our Lady of the Assumption*

The woman clothed with the sun, with the moon under her feet, surrounded by twelve stars: This is also a multidimensional image. Without any doubt, a first meaning is that it is Our Lady, Mary, clothed with the sun, that is, with God, totally; Mary who lives totally in God, surrounded and penetrated by God's light. Surrounded by the twelve stars, that is, by the twelve tribes of Israel, by the whole People of God, by the whole Communion of Saints; and at her feet, the moon, the image of death and mortality. Mary has left death behind her; she is totally clothed in life, she is taken up body and soul into God's glory and thus, placed in glory after overcoming death, she says to us: Take heart, it is love that wins in the end! The message of my life was: I am the handmaid of God, my life has been a gift of myself to God and my neighbor. And this life of service now arrives in real life. May you too have trust and have the courage to live like this, countering all the threats of the dragon.

Homily on the Solemnity of the Assumption
August 15, 2007

44. *The Feast of the Assumption*

The Feast of the Assumption is an invitation to trust in God and also to imitate Mary in what she herself said: Behold, I am the handmaid of the Lord; I put myself at the Lord's disposal. This is the lesson: one should travel on one's own road; one should give life and not take it. And precisely in this way each one is on the journey of love which is the loss of self, but this losing of oneself is in fact the only way to truly find oneself, to find true life. Let us look to Mary, taken up into Heaven. Let us be encouraged to celebrate the joyful feast with faith: God wins. Faith, which seems weak, is the true force of the world. Love is stronger than hate. And let us say with Elizabeth: Blessed are you among women. Let us pray to you with all the Church: Holy Mary, Mother of God, pray for us sinners, now and at the hour of our death. Amen.

Homily on the Solemnity of the Assumption
August 15, 2007

45. *Nearness*

After being taken up into Heaven, Mary did not distance herself from us but continues to be even closer to us and her light shines on our lives and on the history of all humanity. Attracted by the heavenly brightness of the Mother of the Redeemer, let us turn with trust to the One who looks upon us and protects us from on high. We all need her help and comfort to face the trials and challenges of daily life; we need to feel that she is our mother and sister in the concrete situations of our lives. And so that we too may one day be able to share in her same destiny, let us imitate her now in her meek following of Christ and her generous service to the brethren. This is the only way to have a foretaste, already on our earthly pilgrimage, of the joy and peace which those who reach the immortal destination of Paradise live to the full.

Angelus
August 15, 2007

46. *From on high*

May the Virgin Mary, who watches over us from Heaven, help us not to forget that here on earth we are only passing through, and may she teach us to prepare ourselves to encounter Jesus, who is "seated at the right hand of the Father. He will come again in glory to judge the living and the dead."

Angelus
August 12, 2007

X. MOTHER OF THE CHURCH

47. *The Church of the saints*

"Behold, I am the handmaid of the Lord, let it be done to me according to your Word." Mary's reply to the Angel is extended in the Church, which is called to make Christ present in history, offering her own availability so that God may continue to visit humanity with his mercy. The "yes" of Jesus and Mary is thus renewed in the "yes" of the saints, especially martyrs who are killed because of the Gospel.

Angelus
March 25, 2007

48. *In our lives*

It is because she is Mother of the Church that the Virgin is also the Mother of each one of us, members of the Mystical Body of Christ. From the Cross, Jesus entrusted his Mother to all his disciples and at the same time entrusted all his disciples to the love of his Mother. The Evangelist John concludes the brief and evocative account with these words: ". . . And from that hour the disciple took her to his own home" (Jn 19:27). This is the English translation of the Greek text "*eis tá ídia*," he welcomed her into his own reality, his own existence. Thus, she is part of his life and the two lives penetrate each other. And this acceptance of her (*eis tá ídia*) in his own life is the Lord's testament. Therefore, at the supreme moment of the fulfillment of his messianic mission, Jesus bequeaths as a precious inheritance to each one of his disciples his own Mother, the Virgin Mary.

General Audience
January 2, 2008

XI. EUCHARISTIC WOMAN

49. *Masterpiece of grace*

Mary is the "Woman of the Eucharist" par excellence, a masterpiece of divine grace: the love of God has made her immaculate, "holy and blameless before him" (cf. Eph 1:4).

Angelus
March 18, 2007

50. *Eucharist*

Every time we approach the Body and Blood of Christ in the eucharistic liturgy, we also turn to her who, by her complete fidelity, received Christ's sacrifice for the whole Church. The Synod Fathers rightly declared that "Mary inaugurates the Church's participation in the sacrifice of the Redeemer." She is the Immaculata, who receives God's gift unconditionally and is thus associated with his work of salvation.

Apostolic Exhortation The Sacrament of Charity
(Sacramentum Caritatis)*, no. 33*
February 22, 2007

51. *Like Mary*

Mary of Nazareth, icon of the nascent Church, is the model for each of us, called to receive the gift that Jesus makes of himself in the Eucharist.

> *Apostolic Exhortation* The Sacrament of Charity
> (Sacramentum Caritatis), *no. 33*
> *February 22, 2007*

52. *Icon and model*

The Church sees in Mary—"Woman of the Eucharist," as she was called by the Servant of God John Paul II (*Ecclesia de Eucharistia*, no. 53)—her finest icon, and she contemplates Mary as a singular model of the eucharistic life.

> *Apostolic Exhortation* The Sacrament of Charity
> (Sacramentum Caritatis), *no. 96*
> *February 22, 2007*

53. *The Eucharistic Mystery*

May the Virgin Mary, the Woman of the Eucharist, introduce us into the secret of true adoration. Her humble and simple heart was ever pondering the mystery of Jesus, in whom she adored the presence of God and of his redeeming love. May faith in the Eucharistic Mystery, joy in participating in Holy Mass, especially on Sundays, and enthusiasm in witnessing to Christ's immense love grow throughout the Church through her intercession.

Angelus
June 10, 2007

54. *Bringing Sunday into the world*

In today's celebration of the Eucharist, the Son of God has also been given to us. Those who have received Holy Communion, in a special way, carry the Risen Lord within themselves. Just as Mary bore him in her womb—a defenseless little child, totally dependent on the love of his Mother—so Jesus Christ, under the species of bread, has entrusted himself to us, dear brothers and sisters. Let us love this Jesus who gives himself so completely into our hands! Let us love him as Mary loved him! And let us bring him to others, just as Mary brought him to Elizabeth as the source of joyful exultation! The Virgin gave the Word of God a human body, and thus enabled him to come into the world as a man. Let us give our own bodies to the Lord, and let them become ever more fully instruments of God's love, temples of the Holy Spirit! Let us bring Sunday, and its immense gift, into the world!

Angelus
September 9, 2007

55. *Link*

One cannot contemplate Mary without being attracted by Christ and one cannot look at Christ without immediately perceiving the presence of Mary. There is an indissoluble link between the Mother and the Son generated in her womb by the work of the Holy Spirit, and this link we perceive in a mysterious way in the Sacrament of the Eucharist.

Message for the Sixteenth World Day of the Sick
January 11, 2008

XII. Star of Evangelization

56. Model

The Virgin Mary, who did not communicate to the world an idea but Jesus, the Incarnate Word, is an unparalleled model of evangelization.

Angelus
December 23, 2007

57. On a mission

Thanks to the commitment of every believer, the spiritual network of prayer and support for evangelization is being extended throughout the Church. May the Virgin Mary who accompanied with motherly solicitude the development of the newborn Church, also guide our footsteps in our time and obtain for us a new Pentecost of love. May she especially make us all aware of being missionaries, that is, those who have been sent out by the Lord to be his witnesses at every moment of our life.

Message for the Eighty-First World Mission Sunday
May 27, 2007

XIII. ALL-BEAUTIFUL

58. *All-beautiful*

[Mary] is the *tota pulchra*, the all-beautiful, for in her the radiance of God's glory shines forth.

> *Apostolic Exhortation* The Sacrament of Charity
> (Sacramentum Caritatis), *no. 96*
> *February 22, 2007*

59. *Divine fascination*

In contemplation and in activity, in solitude and in fraternity, in service to the poor and the lowly, in personal guidance and in the modern areopaghi, be ready to proclaim and to witness that God is Love and that to love him is sweet. May Mary, the *Tota Pulchra*, teach you to transmit to men and women today this divine fascination that must transpire from your words and actions.

> *Address for the Eleventh World Day of Consecrated Life*
> *February 2, 2007*

60. *Seal*

[Mary], the *Tota Pulchra*, the Virgin Most Pure, who conceived in her womb the Redeemer of mankind and was preserved from all stain of original sin, wishes to be the definitive seal of our encounter with God our Savior. There is no fruit of grace in the history of salvation that does not have as its necessary instrument the mediation of Our Lady.

Homily at Mass for the canonization of St. Anthony of
St. Anne Galvão, Aparecida, Brazil
May 11, 2007

XIV. HUMBLE MOTHER

61. *Gate of Heaven*

If we too want to pass through the narrow door, we must work to be little, that is, humble of heart like Jesus, like Mary his Mother and our Mother. She was the first, following her Son, to take the way of the Cross and she was taken up to Heaven in glory. . . . The Christian people invoke her as *Ianua Caeli*, Gate of Heaven. Let us ask her to guide us in our daily decisions on the road that leads to the "gate of Heaven."

Angelus
August 26, 2007

62. *Encounter of humility*

Here [in Loreto], we think spontaneously of the Holy House of Nazareth, which is the Shrine of humility: the humility of God who took flesh, who made himself small, and the humility of Mary who welcomed him into her womb; the humility of the Creator and the humility of the creature. Jesus, Son of God and Son of man, was born from this encounter of humility. "The greater you are, the more you humble yourself, so you will find favor in the sight of the Lord. For great is the might of the Lord" (3:18-20) says the passage in Sirach; and in the Gospel, after the Parable of the Wedding Feast, Jesus concludes: "Every one who exalts himself will be humbled, and he who humbles himself will be exalted" (Lk 14:11). Today, this perspective mentioned in the Scriptures appears especially provocative to the culture and sensitivity of contemporary man. The humble person is perceived as someone who gives up, someone defeated, someone who has nothing to say to the world. Instead, this is the principal way, and not only because humility is a great human virtue but because, in the first place, it represents God's own way of acting. It was the way chosen by Christ, the Mediator of the New Covenant, who, "being found in human form, he humbled himself and became obedient unto death, even death on a cross" (Phil 2:8).

Homily at Mass in Loreto, Italy
September 2, 2007

XV. Spiritual Mother

63. *Mind and heart*

By learning from Mary, we can understand with our hearts what our eyes and minds do not manage to perceive or contain on their own.

> *Homily on the Solemnity of Mary, Mother of God*
> *January 1, 2007*

64. *Looking to Mary*

Let us look at Mary Most Holy. A humble Handmaid of the Lord, the Virgin is the model of a spiritual person who is totally free because she is immaculate, immune to sin and all holy, dedicated to the service of God and neighbor. May she help us with her motherly care to follow Jesus, to know the truth and to live freedom in love.

> *Angelus*
> *July 1, 2007*

65. *Rediscovering Mary*

Mary . . . remains the Mother of the Word. Rediscovering Mary helps us to make progress as Christians and to come to know the Son.

Lenten meeting with the clergy of Rome
February 22, 2007

66. *Conceiving Christ*

Let us leave space for the word of God which we have the joy of receiving with open and docile hearts, like Mary, Our Lady of the Immaculate Conception, so that, by the power of the Holy Spirit, Christ may once again take flesh in the "today" of our history.

Homily at Mass for the fifth general conference of the
bishops of Latin America and the Caribbean
May 13, 2007

67. *The beauty of conversion*

Let us pray to Mary Most Holy, who accompanies and sustains us on our Lenten journey, so that she may help every Christian to rediscover the greatness, I would say, the beauty, of conversion. May she help us understand that doing penance and correcting one's conduct is not simply moralism, but the most effective way to change oneself and society for the better. An adage expresses it well: to light a candle is worth more than to curse the darkness.

Angelus
March 11, 2007

68. *Like Mary*

Let us ask Mary to teach us how to become, like her, inwardly free, so that in openness to God we may find true freedom, true life, genuine and lasting joy.

Angelus
September 9, 2007

69. *Looking to Jesus*

To look to Jesus with Mary's eyes means encountering God-Love, who for our sake was made man and died on the Cross.

General Audience
September 12, 2007

70. *The dignity of women*

The role of women was important to [St.] Ephrem. The way he spoke of them was always inspired with sensitivity and respect: the dwelling place of Jesus in Mary's womb greatly increased women's dignity. Ephrem held that just as there is no Redemption without Jesus, there is no Incarnation without Mary.

General Audience
November 28, 2007

71. *Guide for young people*

If so many young people want to encounter Mary, and with Mary, Christ, if they let themselves be influenced by the joy of faith, then we can move ahead calmly to meet the future.

Christmas greeting to the members of the Roman Curia
December 21, 2007

72. *Spiritual motherhood*

Mary, in whose virginal womb God was made man, is our Mother! Indeed, from the Cross before bringing his sacrifice to completion, Jesus gave her to us as our Mother and entrusted us to her as her children. This is a mystery of mercy and love, a gift that enriches the Church with fruitful spiritual motherhood. Let us turn our gaze to her, especially today, dear brothers and sisters, and imploring her help, prepare ourselves to treasure all her maternal teaching. Does not our Heavenly Mother invite us to shun evil and to do good, following with docility the divine law engraved in every Christian's heart? Does not she, who preserved her hope even at the peak of her trial, ask us not to lose heart when suffering and death come knocking at the door of our homes? Does she not ask us to look confidently to our future? Does not the Immaculate Virgin exhort us to be brothers and sisters to one another, all united by the commitment to build together a world that is more just, supportive and peaceful?

Prayer at the Spanish Steps for the
Feast of the Immaculate Conception
December 8, 2007

XVI. Mother of Priests

73. *Entrustment to Mary for vocations*

May the Virgin, who promptly answered the call of the Father saying, "Behold, I am the handmaid of the Lord" (Lk 1:38), intercede so that the Christian people will not lack servants of divine joy: priests who, in communion with their Bishops, announce the Gospel faithfully and celebrate the sacraments, take care of the people of God, and are ready to evangelize all humanity. May she ensure, also in our times, an increase in the number of consecrated persons, who go against the current, living the evangelical counsels of poverty, chastity and obedience, and give witness in a prophetic way to Christ and his liberating message of salvation. Dear brothers and sisters whom the Lord calls to particular vocations in the Church: I would like to entrust you in a special way to Mary, so that she, who more than anyone else understood the meaning of the words of Jesus, "My mother and my brethren are those who hear the word of God and do it" (Lk 8:21), may teach you to listen to her divine Son. May she help you to say with your lives: "Lo, I have come to do thy will, O God" (cf. Heb 10:7).

> *Message for the Forty-Fourth World Day of*
> *Prayer for Vocations*
> *February 10, 2007*

74. *Mother of priests*

May Mary, the heavenly Mother of priests, accompany you. May she who beneath the Cross united herself with the Sacrifice of her Son and after the Resurrection accepted together with the other disciples the gift of the Spirit, help you and each one of us, dear brothers in the priesthood, to allow ourselves to be inwardly transformed by God's grace. Only in this way is it possible to be faithful images of the Good Shepherd; only in this way can we carry out joyfully the mission of knowing, guiding and loving the flock which Jesus acquired at the price of his blood.

Homily at Mass for the ordination of new priests for
the Diocese of Rome
April 29, 2007

XVII. Queen of
All Saints

75. *The communion of saints*

The Virgin Mary is resplendent at the center of the Assembly of Saints, "created beings all in lowliness surpassing, as in height, above them all" (Dante, *Paradiso*, Canto XXXIII, 2). By putting our hand in hers, we feel encouraged to walk more enthusiastically on the path of holiness.

Angelus
November 1, 2007

XVIII. QUEEN OF THE FAMILY

76. *The Holy Family*

Today, we are celebrating the Feast of the Holy Family. As we follow the Gospels of Matthew and Luke, let us fix our gaze on Jesus, Mary and Joseph and adore the mystery of a God who chose to be born of a woman, the Blessed Virgin, and to enter this world in the way common to all humankind.

Angelus
December 30, 2007

XIX. QUEEN
OF HEAVEN

77. *The joy of Mary*

The Gospel says nothing about the Mother of the Lord, of Mary, but Christian tradition rightly likes to contemplate her while with joy greater than anyone else's she embraces her divine Son, whom she had held close when he was taken down from the Cross. Now, after the Resurrection, the Mother of the Redeemer rejoices with Jesus' "friends," who constitute the newborn Church. As I renew my heartfelt Easter greetings to you all, I invoke her, the *Regina Caeli* [Queen of Heaven], so that she may keep alive in each one of us faith in the Resurrection and may make us messengers of the hope and love of Jesus Christ.

Regina Caeli
April 9, 2007

XX. Marian
Devotion

78. *Love for Our Lady*

Our Lady, Mother of God, is the Help of Christians, she is our permanent comfort, our great help. . . . Love for Our Lady is the driving force of catholicity. In Our Lady we recognize all God's tenderness, so, fostering and living out Our Lady's, Mary's, joyful love is a very great gift of catholicity.

> *Meeting with clergy of the Dioceses of*
> *Belluno-Feltre and Treviso*
> *July 24, 2007*

79. *The privileges of Mary*

Let us think of the privilege of the "Immaculate Conception," that is, of Mary being immune to sin from conception: she was preserved from any stain of sin because she was to be the Mother of the Redeemer. The same applies to the title "Our Lady of the Assumption": the One who had brought forth the Savior could not be subject to the corruption that derives from original sin. And we know that all these privileges were not granted in order to distance Mary from us but, on the contrary, to bring her close; indeed, since she was totally with God, this woman is very close to us and helps us as a mother and a sister. The unique and unrepeatable position that Mary occupies in the Community of Believers also stems from her fundamental vocation to being Mother of the Redeemer. Precisely as such, Mary is also Mother of the Mystical Body of Christ, which is the Church. Rightly, therefore, on November 21, 1964, during the Second Vatican Council, Paul VI solemnly attributed to Mary the title "Mother of the Church."

General Audience
January 2, 2008

80. *The protection of Mary*

In our day, Our Lady has been given to us as the best defense against the evils that afflict modern life; Marian devotion is the sure guarantee of her maternal protection and safeguard in the hour of temptation.

Homily at Mass for the canonization of St. Anthony of
St. Anne Galvão, Aparecida, Brazil
May 11, 2007

81. *Marian veneration*

She herself, Mother of God, Mother of the Church and our Mother, is present on the various continents, and on different continents she reveals herself as Mother always in the same way, showing her special closeness to every people. I find this very beautiful. She is always Mother of God, she is always Mary, yet she is, so to speak, "inculturated": she has her face, her own special countenance, in Guadalupe, Aparecida, Fatima, Lourdes, in all the countries of the earth. Thus, in this very way she shows herself as Mother: by being close to all. Consequently, all people draw closer to one another through this love for Our Lady. This link which Our Lady creates between continents, between cultures, by being close to each specific culture and at the same time by unifying them all among themselves, seems to me truly important: the whole of the culture's specific features—each has its own richness—is the unity in communion of God's family itself.

Interview during Pope Benedict XVI's flight to Brazil
May 9, 2007

82. *Our Lady of Lourdes*

Today is the Feast of the Blessed Virgin Mary of Lourdes, who a little less than 150 years ago appeared to a simple youth, St. Bernadette Soubirous, showing herself as the Immaculate Conception. Also in that apparition the Blessed Mother has shown herself as a tender mother to her children, recalling that the little, the poor are the beloved of God and to them the mystery of the Kingdom of Heaven is revealed.

Address to the sick at the end of Mass on the
Feast of Our Lady of Lourdes
February 11, 2007

83. *Month of Mary*

The month of May, coinciding at least in part with the Easter Season, is a most favorable time for explaining the figure of Mary as a Mother who accompanies the community of disciples united in prayer in expectation of the Holy Spirit (cf. Acts 1:12-14). This month can thus be an opportunity to return to the faith of the primitive Church and, in union with Mary, to understand that our mission also today is to proclaim and witness with courage and joy to the Crucified and Risen Christ, the hope of humanity.

Regina Caeli
May 6, 2007

84. *Mary, Help of Christians*

May the Virgin Mary, who Don Bosco taught [the Salesians] to call upon as Mother of the Church and Help of Christians, sustain you in your resolutions. "It is she who has done all things," Don Bosco used to repeat at the end of his life, referring to Mary. It will thus once again be Mary who is your guide and teacher.

Letter to the Salesians of Don Bosco for
their general chapter
March 1, 2008

85. *Queen of the most holy Rosary*

The traditional image of Our Lady of the Rosary portrays Mary who with one arm supports the Child Jesus and with the other is offering the rosary beads to St. Dominic. This important iconography shows that the Rosary is a means given by the Virgin to contemplate Jesus and, in meditating on his life, to love him and follow him ever more faithfully.

Angelus
October 7, 2007

86. *Request for protection*

May the Virgin Mary protect us always, both in our mission and in well-deserved rest, so that we may joyfully and fruitfully carry out our work in the Lord's vineyard.

Angelus
July 8, 2007

XXI. Prayers to Mary

Prayer (I)

Mary,
Mother of the "Yes," you listened to Jesus,
and know the tone of his voice
and the beating of his heart.
Morning Star, speak to us of him,
and tell us about your journey of following him
on the path of faith.

Mary,
who dwelt with Jesus in Nazareth,
impress on our lives your sentiments,
your docility, your attentive silence,
and make the Word flourish
in genuinely free choices.

Mary,
speak to us of Jesus,
so that the freshness of our faith
shines in our eyes and warms the heart
of those we meet,

as you did when visiting Elizabeth,
who in her old age rejoiced with you
for the gift of life.

Mary,
Virgin of the *Magnificat*,
help us to bring joy to the world and,
as at Cana, lead every young person
involved in service of others
to do only what Jesus will tell them.

Mary,
look upon the *Agora* of youth,
so that the soil of the Italian Church
will be fertile.
Pray that Jesus, dead and Risen,
is reborn in us,
and transforms us into a night full of light,
full of him.

Mary,
Our Lady of Loreto, Gate of Heaven,
help us to lift our eyes on high.
We want to see Jesus, to speak with him,
to proclaim his love to all.

Prayer at the shrine of Loreto
September 2, 2007

Prayer (II)

Our Mother,
protect the Brazilian
and Latin American family!
Guard under your protective mantle
the children of this beloved land
that welcomes us,
As the Advocate
with your Son Jesus,
give to the Brazilian people constant peace
and full prosperity,
Pour out upon our brothers and sisters
throughout Latin America
a true missionary ardor,
to spread faith and hope,
Make the resounding plea that you uttered in Fatima
for the conversion of sinners
become a reality
that transforms the life of our society,
And as you intercede, from the Shrine of Guadalupe,
for the people
of the Continent of Hope,
bless its lands and its homes,
Amen.

Prayer after the Rosary in Aparecida, Brazil
May 12, 2007

Prayer (III)

Virgin of Nazareth, help us
to be docile to the work
of the Holy Spirit, as you were;
help us to become ever more holy,
disciples in love with your Son Jesus;
sustain and guide these young people
so that they may be joyful
and tireless missionaries of the Gospel
among their peers
in every corner of Italy.
Amen!

Homily at Mass in Loreto, Italy
September 2, 2007

Prayer (IV)

Holy Mary, Immaculate Mother
of our Lord Jesus Christ,
in you God has given us
the model of the Church
and of genuine humanity.
To you I entrust the country of Austria
and its people.
Help all of us to follow your example
and to direct our lives
completely to God!
Grant that, by looking to Christ,
we may become ever more like him:
true children of God! Then we too,
filled with every spiritual blessing,
will be able to conform ourselves more fully
to his will and to become
instruments of his peace
for Austria, Europe and the world. Amen.

Prayer meeting at the Mariensäule, Vienna, Austria
September 7, 2007

Prayer (V): Star of Hope

Teach us, Mary,
to believe, to hope, to love with you;
show us the way that leads to peace,
the way to the Kingdom of Jesus.

You, Star of Hope, who wait for us anxiously
in the everlasting light
of the eternal Homeland, shine upon us
and guide us through daily events,
now and at the hour of our death. Amen!

Prayer at the Spanish Steps for the
Feast of the Immaculate Conception
December 8, 2007

INDEX TO VOLUME ONE

(Numbering refers to the sequential positioning of each thought.)

Love: 20, 28, 75
Marian devotion: 12, 21, 35, 61
Mary:
    advocate, 57
    closeness of, 83, 92, Prayer I
    disciple of Jesus, 59
    dwelling place of God, 14, 19
    dwelling place of the Word, 31, 32, 33
    Epiphany of the Lord, 49
    face of, 1
    heart of, 72, 82
    image of the Son, 64
    in relation with God, 17, 29, 30
    intercession of, 34, 58, Prayer III
    love of the Father, 34, 91
    maternal love of, 39, 55, 66, 68, 83, 91, 98
    model of the Church, 28, 41, 43, 46, 52, 73, 88, 99
    model for prayer, 56, 69, 74, 94, 97
    model of virtue, 85, 90
    Mother of God, 40
    Mother of Jesus, 3, 39
    Mother, our, 51, 66, 67
    praise of, 37, 100
    spiritual mother, 70
    succor, 93, 96
    teacher, 59, 80, 95, Prayer II
    temple of God, 10
    temple of the Holy Spirit, 22, 77, 78, 86
    tent of the Lord, 10, 11
    Woman of the Eucharist, 26, 27, 76
Obedience: 9, 16, 29, 50, 63
Peace: 42
Trinity: 81

INDEX TO VOLUME TWO

(Numbering refers to the sequential positioning of each thought.)

Self-giving: 22, 31, 42-44
Service: 28, 43, 82
Silence: 38
Sorrow: 32
Suffering: 39
Trinity: 29
Truth: 64
Vocation: 73
Woman: 70
Word of God: 3, 66, Prayer I
Young people: 71, Prayer III

RELATED TITLES

Pope Benedict XVI: Spiritual Thoughts

Spiritual Thoughts captures Pope Benedict XVI's spiritual life and his extraordinary intelligence as expressed in the first year of his papacy. His thoughts begin to unlock the mystery of his papal legacy. The short reflections from his talks, homilies, and writings are prayerful, sometimes forceful, and always satisfying. **English: No. 5-765, 128 pp.**

St. Paul
Spiritual Thoughts Series

Unite yourselves with Christ! Let Pope Benedict XVI teach you how to share the gift of Christ with the world like St. Paul did. Every page has a thought from the Pope about St. Paul's life and writings. Use the space in the book to record your own thoughts. Read, grow your biblical literacy, and dive into St. Paul's writings. A book for everyone seeking Christ. **English: No. 7-053, 128 pp.**

The Saints
Spiritual Thoughts Series

Be inspired by Pope Benedict XVI's thoughts about ancient and modern saints. The Holy Father shows how the saints glorified God despite difficulties. Find faith, cling to hope, and learn to love as you read these selections on the saints from the Pope's writings, speeches, and sermons. A book for all Christians. **English: No. 7-055, 128 pp. (est.)**

To order these resources or to obtain a catalog of other USCCB titles, visit *www.usccbpublishing.org* or call toll-free 800-235-8722. In the Washington metropolitan area or from outside the United States, call 202-722-8716. Para pedidos en español, llame al 800-235-8722 y presione 4 para hablar con un representante del servicio al cliente en español.